CATALINA
A *to* Z

CATALINA
A to Z

A GLOSSARY GUIDE TO
California's Island Jewel

PATRICIA MAXWELL, BOB RHEIN
& JERRY ROBERTS

THE
History
PRESS

Published by The History Press
Charleston, SC 29403
www.historypress.net

First published 2014

Manufactured in the United States

ISBN 978.1.60949.774.3

Library of Congress CIP data applied for.

CONTENTS

ACKNOWLEDGEMENTS

Authors of previous publications on Catalina history deserve their share of thanks for paving the way for this book, including but not exclusive to Joe Belanger, Adelaide Le Mert Doran, Alma Overholt, William Sanford White and his writing partners and Jeannine Pedersen. Thanks go to the long memories of Chuck Wright, Natalie Hazard and, especially, community historian Chuck Liddell.

As historical resources have become more of a commodity in the twenty-first century, particularly in California, which continues an intensified investigation into its past, the generosity of people who donate archives and information for the betterment of history and not the bottom line is shrinking. Marvin Carlberg still believes that helping history is the right thing to do. We want to thank him for his solicitude toward the historical record and for his generosity in providing his extensive and rare postcard collection to this project.

We also thank Justin Peter for his excellent photographic skills and donation of time and energy to this project. The staff and management of the Avalon branch of the Los Angeles County Library also helped in directing searches, securing resources and copying documents.

At The History Press, the faith of Brittain Phillips and Adam Ferrell in this project and the guidance and patience of Will McKay and Jaime Muehl have been greatly appreciated.

INTRODUCTION

M ore smugglers, privateers and international flotsam and jetsam might have made Santa Catalina Island a home away from home through the centuries than we may ever know. Contraband was the island's currency in the nineteenth and portions of the twentieth centuries. Cheap labor from China was smuggled through Catalina to the mainland. Later, bootleggers and narcotics traffickers stashed their wares in the island's coves.

The island was traded, swindled, made in payment, picked up for a song and envisioned by many as a dream resort development. The entrepreneurial Banning and then Wrigley families developed the island into what it is today. Hollywood brought bison, yachts and real-life melodrama; Charlie Chaplin, Tom Mix, Errol Flynn, John Wayne, Marilyn Monroe and dozens of others lived their own Catalina escapades. Infamously, Natalie Wood drowned here.

Sport fishing began on Catalina. The first golf course west of the Mississippi River was built on the island. The SS *Catalina*, long the mainland connection for tourists, ended up carrying more people than any other ship in history. Aviation pioneer Glenn Martin made the world's first over-water flight to Catalina from Newport Bay.

General George S. Patton Jr. spent his boyhood summers on Catalina. Western novelist and avid fisherman Zane Grey lived on the island. Wrigley's Chicago Cubs spent the spring training months on Catalina for three decades. Unorthodox naturalist Blanche Trask collected plants here.

Today, the largest for-profit companies on the island are the Santa Catalina Island Company and Southern California Edison, each with its

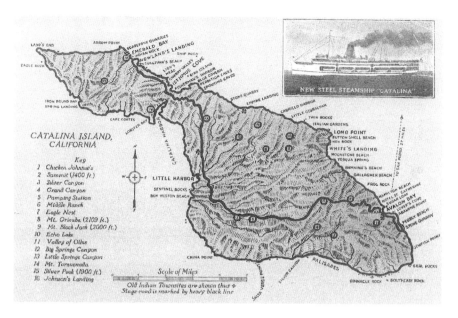

This 1924 souvenir map depicts Santa Catalina Island. Most of the land features remain the same today. *Courtesy of Marvin Carlberg.*

own history and business focus. In 1972, the Wrigley and Offield families set into motion a plan to protect and restore nearly 90 percent of the island by forming the Catalina Island Conservancy. This nonprofit organization is one of California's oldest land trusts.

To have a quick reference for pertinent Catalina facts seemed to us to be a valuable asset for islanders and visitors alike. With travel guides and contemporary tourist references always nearby, that other reference for fast answers with sufficient history still seemed to be absent—until now. This dictionary of events, people, places, superlatives, curiosities and historical subjects provides a needed gap filler for both the casual visitor and the Catalina aficionado. We hope it ends, or starts, some entertaining conversations.

Some overlap occurs between the timeline and the glossary, but it is limited. Our main objective was to provide an easy-to-navigate compilation of quick answers. We made an effort to supply interesting or insightful anecdotes along the way to bring some of these historical characters to life. We also made an effort to have the bibliography be as comprehensive as possible to supplement any Internet search or to send the reader to other sources to get deeper information on specific subjects.

TIMELINE OF CATALINA ISLAND

Miocene epoch	Between five and twenty million years ago, the Farallon and Pacific plates collided and pushed this oceanic island upward from the Pacific Ocean floor to above sea level.
8000 BC	Anthropologists believe humans have occupied the island for some ten thousand years. The early Native American inhabitants were known as Pimaguans or Tongva, later identified as Gabrielinos by circumstance after the Mission San Gabriel near Los Angeles.
October 7, 1542	Sailing for the viceroy of New Spain, explorer Juan Rodríguez Cabrillo landed on the island and named it San Salvador.
November 25, 1602	Explorer Sebastián Vizcaíno renamed the island Santa Catalina in honor of the feast day of Saint Catherine.
March 14–May 1, 1804	Captain and fur trader William Shaler repaired the *Lelia Byrd* at what he called "Port Roussillon," probably Avalon Bay but perhaps Two Harbors.
Early 1800s	Russian and Aleut sea otter hunters, who traded in the Far East, sailed the sea otter–abundant California coast and sojourned on Catalina.

February 18, 1815	The official end of the War of 1812 between the United States and Great Britain caused Spain to close all California ports to foreign vessels, escalating widespread West Coast smuggling by Yankee traders.
1820	New Spain revolted against its mother nation and became Mexico. Alta California (today's California) and Baja California became one province in the new country. Mexicans set tariffs at 100 percent of the value of declared merchandise, and Catalina continued as a smugglers' base of operations.
1820s	The first non–Native American to build a home on Catalina was Samuel Prentiss, a former seaman, sea otter hunter and gold prospector, at Johnsons' Landing, now Emerald Bay, on the island's West End.
Mid-1820s	The last Pimaguans were removed from, or left, the island, some to live at the Mission San Gabriel.
December 1826	Mountain man Jedediah H. Smith, the first individual of European extraction to venture to California via the Rocky Mountains, visited Catalina in the company of Captain William H. Cunningham, who operated a hide-salting operation and lodge at Port Roussellon.
1827	Captain of the *Courier* William H. Cunningham, who had maintained a lodge in what is now Avalon Bay, was ordered by the Mexican government to destroy it as a smugglers' cache, known as Bradshaw's Fort, named for *Franklin* captain John Bradshaw, a contemporary in the smuggling game with Cunningham and others. The "fort," or hide-tannery, stood until at least 1886.
1835	Abel Stearns, future owner of Rancho Los Alamitos and much of the future city of Long Beach, was accused of smuggling at San Pedro, and his warehouse there was linked to smuggling activities at Bradshaw's Fort on Catalina.

1840	Richard Henry Dana's *Two Years Before the Mast* was published; it describes smuggling activities along the Southern California coast.
1843	Ornithologist William Gambel of Philadelphia was the first to collect flora samples on Catalina.
July 4, 1846	Tomas M. Robbins of Santa Barbara was the last recipient of a Mexican land grant in California, from Governor Pío Pico, to use Santa Catalina Island for a home, farm and cattle ranch.
February 2, 1848	The Treaty of Guadalupe Hidalgo ceded Alta California to the United States.
1850	The Thomas Whittley family arrived with their four-year-old son, Frank; a ward named Jose "Mexican Joe" Presciado, age seven; and a herd of sheep. Mexican Joe later served as a goat-hunting guide for several generations and boatman for Charles Frederick Holder and other pioneering sports fishermen of the Tuna Club.
August 31, 1850	Tomas M. Robbins conveyed the island to his friend Santa Barbara rancher Jose Maria Covarrubias for $10,000.
September 9, 1850	California became the thirty-first state in the Union.
1853	One Dr. Creal, who lived on the island for three years, sold Catalina-raised goats at four dollars a head to Pierce & Reed of San Francisco. Catalina was used as a smuggling way station for contraband Chinese laborers illegally entering the United States to build the Transcontinental Railroad.
October 13, 1853	Jose Covarrubias, who deemed Catalina an "ugly wart," deeded the island to Santa Barbara attorney Albert Packard for $1,000.
1854	The island's first permanent, non–Native American resident, Samuel Prentiss, died and was buried on a hill above Johnsons' Landing, now Emerald Bay.

1854	The Johnson (aka Johnston) brothers, John L. and James Charles, arrived on Catalina and built a horse and sheep ranch just west of Johnsons' Landing.
1857	Louisa Behn Stoll (1857–1935) was born to lumber schooner captain John Behn and his wife at the Behn Ranch. She is believed to have been the first non–Native American—or, in the parlance of the times, "white"—child born on the island.
1858	Captain William Howland and his wife settle on the West End at the place that bears his name: Howland's Landing.
June 9, 1858	Albert Packard sold one-fourth of the island to Eugene Sullivan for $500.
1859	General Phineas Banning led a yachting party of potential investors and partners to the island.
Early 1860s	A Catalina Island "gold rush" uncovered negligible amounts of the precious metal.
1863	Eugene Sullivan sold his island property to Dr. C.M. Hitchcock for $1,864.
	A barracks was built for Union troops at Puerto de Santa Catalina, later renamed Isthmus Cove.
November 26, 1863	Union lieutenant James F. Curtis reported his findings on the island. Of the one hundred residents, half were miners. About fifteen thousand sheep and eight thousand goats grazed the island. Named residents included brothers Charles and John Johnson, Francisco Guerrero, William Howland, Spencer Wilson, the Whittley family, Benjamin Weston, Juan Cota and D.B. Dietz.
1864	A company of Union soldiers explored the island for use as an Indian reservation, a plan that was abandoned.
January 1, 1864	The island became a Union military possession, declared by the Fourth Infantry of the California Volunteers.
May 14, 1864	James H. Ray of New York purchased the island from Packard and Covarrubias for $12,500.

May 23, 1864	Nine days after buying the island, James H. Ray sold half of it for $4,150 to Pennsylvania manufacturer and philanthropist James Lick, who was then residing near San Francisco.
September 20, 1864	A letter from John Johnson appeared in the San Francisco newspaper *Daily Alta California* reporting that the soldiers and miners had left the island.
May 23, 1865	C.M. Hitchcock sold his one-fourth interest to James Lick for $15,000.
December 4, 1865	The U.S. District Court at Monterey decided to discontinue the open-ended Robbins-Covarrubias appeal to own the island after an investigation by J. Tyler Jr. and his report to U.S. attorney general Caleb Cushing presuming fraud in the case.
April 8, 1866	William Percival Howland was the first non–Native American male child born on the island, the second son of cattleman William Howland.
June 26, 1866	Los Angeles County sheriff T.A. Sanchez sold all of James H. Ray's interests in the island to one Crockett for $1,526.56. Crockett sold the interests back to Ray for the exact same price, $1,525.56. This partial information points to continued fraud.
1867	Stephen Bouchey bought Dr. C.M. Hitchcock's mine on the island for $7,000.
September 16, 1867	James Lick bought the last remaining property on the island that wasn't already his from Walter Hawxhurst of Contra Costa County for $4,140. Lick paid a total of $92,000 for the island.
1868–72	*Lick v. Howland et al.* was a legal effort to evict the island's squatters, many of whom had lived on Catalina for generations. Named in the suit were B.D.S. Diltz, Nat Narbonne, Lawson Swain, M.W. Grady, S. Boushey, Thomas O'Hara, William Howland, Thomas Gallagher, Francisco Guerrera, John L. Johnson, S.W. Wilson and C. Sawyer, among more than twenty other names, including William Walker, Mark Twain and John Bull.

1870s	Paul Schumacher conducted archaeological investigations on Catalina for the Smithsonian Institute.
1870s/early 1880s	James Lick died in 1876, and the Lick Estate trustees granted grazing rights to William Howland, Harris and Whittley.
1880s	Only one person supposedly lived permanently on Catalina after the Union soldiers' eviction of the miners during the Civil War and Lick's successful eviction suit: John Sullivan. He was characterized by one writer as an escaped convict who resided in a cabin at Isthmus Cove.
1884–85	W.S. Lyon and Reverend C.J. Nevin made an extensive flora exploration of Catalina. A federally endangered petite yellow pygmy daisy was rediscovered on Catalina in 2011. Its scientific name, *Pentachaeta lyonii*, is for Lyon, who first collected the flower in 1884.
1886	Chris L. Ringsen (born in March 1860 in Denmark) and D. Fenton established Catalina's first boat rental business in front of the location where the Hotel Metropole was going to be built on the future Avalon Bay front.
August 11, 1887	James Lick's trustees sold the island to George R. Shatto and silent partner, C.A. Sumner, for $200,000.

1887–91	The hunting lodge or smuggler's cache that probably had been William Shaler's "Port Roussellon" and later a collection of shacks that Mexican authorities glorified in reports as "Bradshaw's Fort" was, for brief periods, known as Sachem Bay, Johnston's Landing (confusing, since Johnson's Landing was on the West End near Emerald Bay) and Timms Landing or Timms Cove after San Pedro trader Augustus Timms. The place endured on maps for several generations as Dakin's Cove or Dankin's Cove, nomenclature that remains a mystery. It was briefly renamed Shatto, after its new owner George R. Shatto, when he platted the town. Etta Marilla Whitney (February 3, 1862–March 27, 1950), Shatto's sister-in-law, is said to have come up with the name Avalon for Timms Landing. Her inspiration was taken from Alfred Lord Tennyson's poem "Idylls of the King."
October 13, 1888	Shatto and Sumner's Hotel Metropole in Avalon held its grand opening. Promotional materials announcing the hotel left out the *l*, so on the island and mainland, the new structure was known as the "Metropoe."
February 5, 1889	The Agassiz Society, Chapter A, No. 861, was formed in Avalon with eighteen members, organized by Mrs. Sophia A. Wheeler (b. 1838), Avalon's first teacher, for the purpose of collecting and discussing "natural objects of facts" and discussing natural history, science, biography and historic literature. The meetings were held in the Avalon Home, which doubled as the Wheeler Hotel and Bakery on Crescent Avenue, site of the present Lloyd's. Louis Agassiz was a notable globetrotting naturalist.

February 26, 1889	The SS *Hermosa*, a 141-foot wooden ship with a passenger capacity of 150, made its maiden voyage for the Wilmington Transportation Company from San Pedro to Avalon. The *Hermosa* was the first long-operating Catalina–mainland transport—for fourteen years.
1889	A topographical survey of the island was made by the U.S. Coast and Geodetic Survey.
April 26, 1889	Shatto sold the mineral rights to the island to International Mining Syndicate Ltd., of London, for $400,000.
June 13, 1889	Avalon's first homicide was the accidental shooting death of sixteen-year-old Laura E. Pock at the Avalon shooting range of Conrad S. Miller. His Winchester rifle discharged when he turned it over on the counter, and it killed the girl, who was in a rented tent behind the gallery.
July 27, 1889	Harry Minto Alexander Elms (December 31, 1866–January 27, 1962), Catalina's first postmaster, established the island's U.S. Post Office in his seashell store on the beach in Avalon. The mail was delivered twice a week on the sail ship *Ida*.
1889	The first church was built in Avalon. It was the Congregational Church, known today as the Avalon Community Church.
December 1889	International Mining Syndicate Ltd. ceased to exist in an English court, according to a law that said if a corporation fails to meet obligations, it is dissolved. The Shatto contract was null and void.
1890	On land bought from George Shatto for $500 on the slope of the southern hill overlooking Avalon Bay, Peter Gano finished his conspicuous dream castle, called Look Out Cottage and known today as Holly Hill House.

December 30, 1891	After defaulting on his mortgage to the Lick Estate, Shatto sold the island and his interests there to J.B. Banning for $1.
1892	The Banning brothers—J.B., Hancock and William—followed through on what Shatto could not, and Avalon experienced its greatest building boom year. The Bannings made major improvements to the Hotel Metropole, Steamer Pier, water and sewage systems and streets. They built the Glenmore Hotel/Restaurant, Hotel Catalina and Grand View Hotel—all in Avalon. Locals and investors followed that lead, building or opening up the Sunset Home/Apartments, Old Maids Inn, Mathewson Cottages, Leneta Hotel, Spanish Hotel and Restaurant, Miramar Hotel and Alhambra Hotel/Aloha Hotel, as well as various camps and stores.

After George Shatto purchased the island from the Lick Estate, he constructed Avalon's first hotel, the Hotel Metropole. The Banning brothers built on to the existing building from 1892 to 1918. *Courtesy of Marvin Carlberg.*

1892	The Catalina Yacht Club, organized by the Bannings, was formed in Avalon.
	Captain J.E. "Pard" Mathewson opened the Avalon Boat Works, a boatbuilding and repair shop.
	The Catalina Country Club was founded with the first golf course in Southern California, a three-hole affair on the sand.
	The *Jewfish*, the first island newspaper, was published.
August 1892	F.A. Seavey made the first collection of Catalina insects.
September 20, 1892	William Banning, son of transportation pioneer Phineas Banning, paid the Lick Estate the remainder of Shatto's bill, $128,740. Shatto died in a train wreck in the western Mojave Desert.
1893	The short-lived *Avalon Avalanche* newspaper was published.
1894	Dr. O.T. Fellows built a stone inn at Little Harbor as a stop on the primitive road from Avalon to Two Harbors.
	The first Catalina Island–mainland communication system consisted of carrier pigeons. From 1894 to 1898, Otto J. and Oswald Zahn conducted a pigeon mail service between Avalon and Bunker Hill in downtown Los Angeles.
October 16, 1894	The Banning brothers formed the Santa Catalina Island Company, Inc., to operate their interests on the island.
1896	Eagle's Nest Lodge, located in Middle Ranch Canyon on the Pacific side of the island, was built by Daniel A. Baughman as an inn, stagecoach stop and hunting lodge.
May 7, 1896	William Banning deeded the island to the Santa Catalina Island Company. The stockholders were himself; his brothers, Joseph B. and Hancock Banning; and their two sisters.

The Farnsworth Loop is seen along the Stagecoach Road out of Avalon. Samuel S. Farnsworth began building a road from Avalon to the isthmus for the Banning Company on March 20, 1897, using picks and shovels. The road was completed about June 1, 1898. The loop was considered a masterpiece of engineering in the days of the stagecoach. *Courtesy of Marvin Carlberg.*

March 20, 1897	Samuel S. Farnsworth began construction on the official Stagecoach Road from Avalon to Two Harbors.
1898	The Tuna Club, the oldest fishing club in the United States, was founded in Avalon by Charles Frederick Holder and other sport-fishing enthusiasts.
June 1, 1898	The Stagecoach Road, aka Stage Road, from Avalon to Two Harbors was completed.
1899	The Banning Aquarium, with fifty tanks displaying sea life, was built on the Avalon waterfront in collaboration with naturalist Charles Frederick Holder.
1900	Avalon was characterized as a "tent city" with a summer population of three thousand and a year-round population of one hundred.

George Shatto assumed island ownership in 1867, laid out streets and sold lots to vacationers. Vacation rentals in those days were striped tourist tents along the tree-lined neighborhoods of Avalon. Each summer starting in 1887, the Bannings lined sections of Clarissa, Catalina and Sumner Avenues with tent housing. Accommodations ranged from two-person tents that were seven square feet to large "marquees" with living rooms and four bedrooms. *Courtesy of Marvin Carlberg.*

The bathhouse near the location of the present-day Tuna Club was the hub of watersports activities, circa 1900s. *Courtesy of Marvin Carlberg.*

1901	The first school, a two-room structure, was built in Avalon. Regular school classes had been held in Avalon since 1891, first under the tutelage of a Mrs. Morris in the Congregational Church.
1902	Communication with the mainland was improved by the Pacific Wireless Company station, the world's first such wireless communication facility.
	The SS *Hermosa II* replaced the SS *Hermosa* as the main vessel carrying passengers to and from Catalina. The *Hermosa II* had a passenger capacity of seven hundred. The Wilmington Transportation Company boat operated regularly until 1920.
	Experimenting with glass-bottomed rowboats, Pard Mathewson built the first glass-bottomed side-wheeler, the thirty-eight-foot *Mon Ami*, the first of the touring glass-bottomed boats.
August 12, 1902	The noted "Hotel Metropole Murder" occurred. This was the fatal shooting of W.A. "the St. Louis Sport" Yeager, after a night of illegal gambling in a back room of Avalon's landmark hotel. The still-open case went cold when Alfred Boyd was acquitted of the killing.
1903	The *Avalon Crusoe*, another short-lived newspaper, was published.
March 25, 1903	The *Wireless* newspaper, owned by Willis Lefavor, began publishing in Avalon as the world's first newspaper that received its news via a wireless device.
August 19, 1903	The Santa Catalina Island Company borrowed $1 million to pay off a debt of $98,348.46 to the California Academy of Sciences and to make improvements on the island to infrastructure, utilities, et cetera.

The pride of the Bannings' fleet was the SS *Cabrillo*, built at the brothers' own shipyard at the Port of Los Angeles and christened in 1904. It carried six hundred passengers. The *Cabrillo* plied the channel between San Pedro and Avalon until it was sold to the U.S. government as a troop ship in World War II. *Courtesy of Marvin Carlberg.*

1904	The Wilmington Transportation Company added the SS *Cabrillo* to its fleet, and it joined the SS *Hermosa II* on the Catalina run. Able to carry 1,200 passengers and with ten staterooms, this 194-foot vessel operated for more than four decades.
1904–5	With the Banning brothers' backing, island resident Dr. Lee DeForest developed the Audion vacuum tube, patented in 1907 and essential to radio technology, revolutionizing twentieth-century communication.
1906	The tunnel from Avalon to Descanso Bay through Sugarloaf, a giant rock formation on the west side of Avalon Harbor, collapsed, altering Sugarloaf into two formations: Big Sugarloaf and Little Sugarloaf.

On August 11, 1906, the Bannings opened the Intermountain Railway to carry passengers up the steep hill that later was named Mount Ada by the Wrigleys. This short line ran from near the Amphitheater, at a 30 percent grade, uphill to Buena Vista Park at an elevation of about three hundred feet. A slightly shorter, steeper spur ran down to Lovers Cove, where the glass-bottomed boats docked. The Intermountain Railway ceased operation in 1918 due to lack of tourism following the 1915 fire. *Courtesy of Marvin Carlberg*

August 11, 1906	The Intermountain Railroad, a sightseeing operation south of Avalon over Buena Vista Peak and down to Lovers Cove and back, was opened by the Bannings.
July 4, 1908	The *Catalina Daily Mirror* newspaper began publishing for the summer.
1909	Permanent Avalon residents numbered about five hundred, and the summer population swelled to ten thousand.

Avalon, circa 1909. A wooden boardwalk linked the two piers. The then-unincorporated town consisted of about five hundred year-round residents and swelled to ten thousand folks during the summer seasons. *Courtesy of Marvin Carlberg.*

1909	The eventual 407-foot Pleasure Pier, later known as the Green Pleasure Pier, was built and maintained by the Santa Catalina Island Company.
1910	A Model T Ford owned by Allan Hancock blazed a trail from Avalon to Two Harbors in four hours.
	Judge J.B. Banning, the middle Banning brother, built his large hacienda on a knoll overlooking the Isthmus at Two Harbors.
	The first motion picture shot on the island was the ten-minute *Feeding Seals at Catalina Isle.*
1912	Director D.W. Griffith's *Man's Genesis* was filmed on Catalina, one of the first of hundreds of Hollywood feature productions filmed on the island.

A view of the Hotel Metropole and steamer pier when the Bannings owned the island. Tied up to the pier is the SS *Hermosa*. *Courtesy of Marvin Carlberg.*

May 10, 1912	Glenn L. Martin flew a pontoon-equipped, box-kite flying machine from Newport Bay to Catalina—thirty-four miles in thirty-seven minutes—in the longest over-water flight up to that time with the first on-water landing.
1913	Through the efforts of naturalist Charles F. Holder, the California legislature passed a law making Catalina's near-shore waters a fish reservation.
June 19, 1913	Avalon incorporated as Los Angeles County's thirtieth city by a vote of 132 to 82.
January 27, 1914	The *Catalina Islander* was first published to promote the Santa Catalina Island Company. It was edited for thirty-eight years by Ernest Windle.
1915	Pard Mathewson brought the first commercial automobile to Avalon to deliver coal oil and gasoline.
November 29, 1915	A devastating fire destroyed most of Avalon.

1916	Ralph Glidden excavated Native American sites at Johnsons' Landing, known today as Empire Landing, as well as at Howland's Landing, Little Harbor and White's Cove.
1917	Big Sugarloaf, the rock formation between Avalon and Descanso Bay, was blasted away to make room for Sugarloaf Casino.
1918	The luxurious Hotel St. Catherine, built by the Banning brothers in the gardens of Hancock Banning's residence, was completed off Descanso Bay. The Intermountain Railroad closed for business. It operated sporadically as late as 1921 and was dismantled in 1923.
1919	Chaplin Air Line, operated by Charlie Chaplin's half-brother, Sydney, began seaplane service to Catalina from Wilmington with Curtiss MF Seagull flying boats.
February 1919	William Wrigley Jr. gained controlling interest in the Santa Catalina Island Company by purchasing the Banning interests for $3 million.
1920s	Lead, silver, copper and zinc were mined by the Wrigley interests and overseen by David Renton with shipments to smelters at Selby, California, and in Europe.
1920	The Pacific Telephone Company opened a wireless radiotelephone system for mainland communication.
April 11, 1920	Wrigley's purchase of the Santa Catalina Island Company included the Wilmington Transportation Company, to which he added the SS *Virginia*, renaming it the SS *Avalon*. The 264-foot *Avalon*'s maiden voyage on the Catalina run occurred on this date, and it served Catalina for thirty-one years.
1921	Al Jolson's "Avalon," which he co-wrote and which was a virtual advertisement for the resort town, rose to number two on the charts.

The entrance to William and Ada Wrigley's residence, Mount Ada. The home was built in 1921. It was converted to a bed-and-breakfast, the Inn at Mount Ada, in August 1985. *Photo by Justin Peter.*

	The Wrigley mansion, later the Inn at Mount Ada, on the hilltop south of Avalon, was completed by William Wrigley Jr.
	The first radio station on Catalina was the crystal set in Lawrence Mott's home.
1921	Peter Gano's three-thousand-square-foot, three-floor residence, Look Out Cottage, was sold to the Giddings family, who changed the structure's name to Holly Hill House.
	William Wrigley Jr. bought a controlling interest in the Chicago Cubs, and the team used the island for spring training from this date through 1952.
	A heavy freight wharf was built on the Avalon side of Sugarloaf and supplied the island for thirty-seven years.
1922	Al Bombard's Catalina Speedboat Company began operations, making "Miss Catalina" craft.

1923	Telephone communications improved when cables were placed on the ocean floor between Avalon and San Pedro.
	Despite Prohibition, the *Islander* reported one thousand cases of whiskey cached on the beach near Eagle Rock.
January 1923	Publication of *The Flora of Santa Catalina Island* by Charles Frederic Millspaugh and Lawrence William Nutall, by the Department of Botany at Chicago's Field Museum of Natural History, detailed the island's plants.
1924	Built by William Wrigley Jr. at a cost of $1 million, the 301-foot SS *Catalina* began service to and from Avalon and San Pedro.
	Thompson Dam and water system was completed. The fresh water was pumped to Wrigley Reservoir above Avalon and then gravity fed to the town.
March 27, 1924	The Catalina Yacht Club incorporated in Los Angeles.
June 12, 1924	On maneuvers between Santa Catalina and San Clemente Islands, the battleship USS *Mississippi* experienced two explosions in its gun turrets, killing forty-eight sailors.
December 24, 1924	Fourteen American bison were brought to the Isthmus by Famous Players–Lasky, a film production company, and set free to roam the wild lands.
1925	The Chimes Tower was built by Mrs. Ada Wrigley on a hill on the north side of Avalon Bay and has rung on the quarter hour between 8:00 a.m. and 8:00 p.m. ever since.
	William Wrigley Jr. engaged John Duncan Dunn to build a golf course at White's Landing. Dunn found 267 skeletons, presumably part of a Native American burial ground. The bones were supposedly shipped to the Museum of the Heye Foundation in New York.

1925	The Boy Scouts of America leased Emerald Bay for the first time.
1926	*Margaret C.*, a schooner, was blown up for a movie shoot in Catalina Harbor.
1926	Western novelist Zane Grey built his residence, which since has been converted into the Zane Grey Pueblo Hotel, on the north hillside above Avalon Harbor.
February 17, 1926	The *S.N. Castle*, a barquentine or sailing vessel with three or more sails, was burned and sunk in Catalina Harbor for director James Cruze's film *Old Ironsides*, the first big-budget picture filmed on Catalina, starring Wallace Beery.
1927	William Wrigley Jr.'s son, P.K. Wrigley, built his mansion, Casa del Monte, on Sunshine Terrace above Avalon. The price of metals fell off, and Wrigley suspended mining operations.

Philip Knight Wrigley, who guided island interests via the Santa Catalina Island Company through the mid-twentieth century, built his home, Casa del Monte, on Sunshine Terrace on the north side hill of Avalon. *Courtesy of Marvin Carlberg.*

1927	Catalina Clay Products, a division of Wrigley's Santa Catalina Island Company, opened to take advantage of island clay deposits, produce building materials and provide residents with year-round employment.
January 15, 1927	Canadian George Young became the first documented person to swim the Catalina Channel. His time was fifteen hours, forty-four minutes and thirty seconds.
1928	In the forerunner of what became the Catalina Classic Paddleboard Race, Tom Blake won the island's first mainland surfing and paddleboard competition on a 120-pound board. He broke every paddleboard record that previously existed.
October 3, 1928	The *Dauntless*, a schooner, was blown up off Catalina Harbor for director Herbert Brenon's film *The Rescue*, starring Ronald Colman and surfing legend Duke Kahanamoku.
1929	The *Charles F. Crocker*, a barquentine, was run aground and dismasted for a movie shoot, and the wreck later washed ashore.
May 29, 1929	The grand opening of the new Catalina Island Casino, designed by Los Angeles architects Weber and Spaulding, included much pomp and circumstance.
September 22, 1929	On a U.S. vacation, future British prime minister Winston Churchill hooked a 188-pound marlin off Catalina and reeled it in less than twenty minutes.
December 13, 1930	The *Valiant*, a 162-foot-long, 444-ton, steel luxury yacht, caught fire from an engine-room gaffe in Descanso Bay, burned for three days and then sank in 110 feet of water.
1931	The Santa Catalina Island Company operated a fleet of five glass-bottomed boats at Avalon.

August 1, 1931	Catalina Airport, with a concrete ramp for the Wrigleys' Wilmington–Catalina Airline seaplanes to roll out of the surf, officially opened in Hamilton Cove.
1932	Philip K. Wrigley selected a spot near Cottonwood Canyon to construct El Rancho Escondido, a 538-acre Arabian horse ranch.
January 26, 1932	William Wrigley Jr. died in Arizona of acute indigestion. His son, Philip K. Wrigley, became director of the Santa Catalina Island Company.
1933	The Wrigley Memorial was completed in Avalon Canyon. William Wrigley Jr. was interred there.
1934	Robert Louis Stevenson's *Treasure Island*, starring Jackie Cooper and Wallace Beery as Long John Silver, was filmed by director Victor Fleming at Catalina Harbor and Emerald Bay.
November 12, 1934	Eight men, employees of Rohl-Connoly (today's Connoly-Pacific), were killed in an accidental explosion of black powder at the East End quarry.
Mid-1930s	Catalina's rock quarries sent massive quantities of stone to build the Santa Monica breakwater and Newport Beach Harbor.
1935	Director Frank Lloyd shot many scenes at Two Harbors for perhaps Catalina's most famous film, the Academy Award–winning best picture *Mutiny on the Bounty*, starring Clark Gable and Charles Laughton.
1937	Catalina Clay Products ceased operations after a decade.
1938	The *Ning Po*, the 1753 vintage Chinese junk that survived rebellion and piracy through a long career, burned in Catalina Harbor in a fire that destroyed other vessels, including the *Lewellyn J. Morse*. The *Ning Po* had long been regarded as the oldest ship afloat. It had been in California since 1913 and off Catalina since 1917.

Built in 1753, the *Ning Po* spent 159 years engaged in smuggling, slave trading, mutiny and piracy. The number of people killed aboard the vessel hasn't been tallied, but it's said that 158 heads rolled on the decks. Launched in 1753 in the city of Fu Chau as a three-masted, 291-ton junk named the *Kin Tai Foong*, this 138-footer was built entirely of camphor and ironwood. No nails were used. The *Ning Po* was beached and later burned in 1938. *Courtesy of Marvin Carlberg.*

1938	The *Palmyra*, a schooner, was beached and burned at Catalina Island.
1939	*Kay Kyser's Kollege of Musical Knowledge*, broadcasted over the NBC Radio Network, originated for the first time from the Casino at Avalon.
1941	The Santa Catalina Island Company merged with the Fleming and Weber Company, with the former name surviving as the official concern.
June 20, 1941	Universal Pictures released director Charles Lamont's B-musical *San Antonio Rose*, starring Jane Frazee, Eve Arden and Lon Chaney Jr. and featuring the song "Hi, Neighbor." Jack Owens, a pop singer known as the "Cruisin' Crooner" on Don McNeill's *Breakfast Club* over the NBC Blue Radio Network, wrote the music and lyrics for the song after hearing the phrase bellowed by Duke Fishman so often on visits to Catalina.

1941–45	The island joined the war effort, generally suspending resort operations and sending sons and daughters, as well as former commercial vessels, into the armed services. The U.S. Maritime Service, Coast Guard and Office of Strategic Services, as well as the army and navy, used the island for training, coast watching and deployment.
July 27, 1942	Republic Pictures released Charles Lamont's B-musical *Hi, Neighbor*, starring Jean Parker and based on the Catalina-inspired hit pop song by Jack Owens.
October 17, 1944	The U.S. Navy blimp *K-111* crashed on Catalina, killing six of the ten crewmen.
May 1946	Microwave radiophone technology by the Pacific Telephone Company was put into use at Pebbly Beach, supplementing submarine cable circuits. It was the first public use of microwave technology, which was utilized by the military in World War II.
June 27, 1946	The Airport in the Sky officially opened at Buffalo Springs. United Airlines operated DC-3s from three California cities to Catalina.

Once located at the Hamilton Cove seaplane airport, this hangar was brought up to the Airport in the Sky in the late 1960s to house Philip Knight Wrigley's DC-3. *Photo by Justin Peter.*

August 1946	John O'Dea's *The Gentle Approach*, the first legitimate stage play mounted on Catalina, was underwritten by the Theater Production Guild, staged in the Avalon Theater and starred Robert Mitchum and Jacqueline De Wit.
December 14, 1946	William Wrigley Jr.'s remains were removed from the Wrigley Memorial for interment at Forest Lawn in Glendale, California.
1950	The tourist attraction Submarine Diving Bell, which held a dozen people and showcased life beneath the surf, was introduced at Casino Point. It ceased operations in 1961 and was removed to the Steel Pier at Atlantic City, New Jersey.
1951	The *Davy Jones Show*, a live Santa Catalina Island Company marine tourism attraction in Lovers Cove, was centered on a fifty-one-foot barge with beneath-the-surface windows. It ceased operations in 1963. Mart Toggweiler began steady operation from San Pedro in Catalina waters of the first regular West Coast dive boat, the *Maray*, crafted from a navy surplus landing craft.
1952	Radio station KBIG went on the air with transmitters near Avalon, and Carl "Mr. Big" Bailey, a tall drink of water, was its on-air personality. Bailey became an in-demand emcee around town.
September 21, 1952	Florence Chadwick became the first woman, tenth person and second-fastest swimmer to swim the Catalina Channel, with a time of thirteen hours, forty-two minutes and thirty-two seconds.
1953	The University of California Los Angeles began archaeological surveys and excavations on Catalina Island. The Santa Catalina Island Museum Society incorporated to preserve the island's unique cultural heritage.

This souvenir brochure of Catalina Island dates to 1951. Avalon is a city built for tourism, and in recent decades, Catalina has received nearly one million annual visitors. *Courtesy of Marvin Carlberg.*

July 1954	Mart Toggweiler speared a 203-pound black sea bass at Goat Harbor, breaking the world's black sea bass spear-fishing record by 50 pounds.
August 22, 1954	Zale Parry broke the women's deep-sea-diving record three miles out of Avalon by descending from the workboat *Weasel* to the ocean floor at 209 feet.
1957	After advances in the aqualung, the 1943 deep-water-diving device invented by Jacques-Yves Cousteau and Emile Gagnan, construction began in Avalon on Catalina Divers Supply, the first dive shop on Catalina.
	The television adventure show *Sea Hunt*, based at Marineland on Palos Verdes Peninsula, used Catalina waters for many location episodes. Star Lloyd Bridges's double, Courtney Brown, and stuntwoman Zale Parry performed the Catalina dives. *Sea Hunt* ceased production in 1961.
1958	The heavy freight landing point for barges and other craft was moved from Casino Point to Pebbly Beach.
	The pop song "26 Miles (Santa Catalina)" by the Four Preps reached number two on the Billboard Hot 100 chart and number six on the Billboard R&B chart. The Four Preps sang the island's biggest musical recognition live on CBS's *The Ed Sullivan Show* the same year.
October 5, 1958	Greta Anderson became the first person to swim the Catalina Channel and then swim back after nearly a half-hour rest. Her total time was twenty-six hours, fifty-three minutes and twenty-eight seconds.
August 6, 1959	The Santa Catalina Island Company reincorporated and restated business purposes, most related to maintaining the island infrastructure and promoting island tourism.

September 20, 1959	The original California Outrigger Classic, presided over by Grand Marshal Duke Kahanamoku, a Hawaii surfing legend, traveled from Avalon across the channel to Newport Dunes.
July 18, 1960	The SS *Avalon*, nearly a decade removed from Catalina service, caught fire and burned at the Port of Long Beach.
1962	Southern California Edison took ownership of Avalon's utilities, specifically fresh water, gas and electricity. Edison's natural gas and diesel fuel depot was at Pebbly Beach.
December 3, 1962	In a Shell Oil–financed experiment using special gases, the diving bell Atlantis descended to the ocean floor at 1,028 feet off Catalina to prove such dives could facilitate oil recovery. British photojournalist Peter Small and backup safety diver Chris Whitaker were killed in the attempt.
January 18, 1964	The Catalina Channel Balloon Race took off from old Wrigley Field and included such participants as actor Cliff Robertson and stunt pilot Frank Tallman. Barbara Keith, the lone female balloonist, never reached land. Her body was found the next day off San Onofre. She had gone down in the water and died of hypothermia.
1965	An underwater diving park was created off Casino Point.
March 8, 1965	Philip K. Wrigley transferred the deed to forty-five acres at Big Fisherman's Cove to the University of Southern California for the construction of a marine science center.
1966	Once a world-class luxury accommodation, the Hotel St. Catherine was torn down in Descanso Canyon.

Kids in Avalon earned extra money by diving for coins when passenger steamers would dock. The divers cached the coins in their mouths. An enterprising youngster could collect forty dollars a day. This postcard is dated 1909. Diving for coins continued until the 1960s, when the steamer pier was removed. *Courtesy of Marvin Carlberg.*

June 9, 1966	Metro-Goldwyn-Mayer released director Frank Tashlin's romantic comedy *The Glass Bottom Boat*, starring Doris Day, Rod Taylor and Arthur Godfrey. Set in Avalon and concerning a major Catalina recreation feature, the film remains one of the most notable Catalina hits in pop culture.
1967	Construction began on the University of Southern California's Marine Science Center in Big Fisherman's Cove.
December 1967	The B-picture *Catalina Caper*, set and filmed on the island, starred Tommy Kirk in a Clyde Ware story of swinging teens foiling crooks. The picture was later satirized on *Mystery Science Theatre 3000*.
1968	The big steamer pier was removed from Avalon Bay, and more yacht moorings were added.

December 12, 1968	Judge Ernest Windle, who had been the justice for the Santa Catalina–San Clemente Island Justice Court, passed away at eighty-nine. He had been the oldest serving judge in California.
January 1971	Richard M. Nixon became the second sitting U.S. president, after Calvin Coolidge, to visit Catalina.
1972	The Brown Berets, Latino activists, attempted to seize the island in Mexico's name, citing the Treaty of Guadalupe Hidalgo, the 1848 United States–Mexico agreement that ceded Alta California (today's California) to the States. The treaty never mentioned islands. The commotion ceased bloodlessly.
	The Santa Catalina Island Conservancy was formed by the Wrigley and Offield families to protect the island's wild lands in perpetuity, eventually governing 88 percent of the island as one of the oldest land trusts in California.
1974	The Santa Catalina Island Company signed a fifty-year easement agreement with Los Angeles County, ensuring public use of the land managed by the newly formed conservancy.
June 20, 1974	Paramount Pictures released director Roman Polanski's private eye classic *Chinatown*, starring Jack Nicholson, Faye Dunaway and John Huston, with a key scene set on Catalina during lunch at the "Albacore Club."
Mid-1970s	The alcoholic drink called Buffalo Milk was created at Two Harbors. No bison, of course, were milked to produce the drink.
1975	The SS *Catalina* was retired from passenger service, having carried more people than any other boat anywhere, according to the Steamship Historical Society of America.
	The statue of Old Ben, the famous sea lion that had been an Avalon Harbor habitué up until 1921, was dedicated on the end of the Cabrillo Mole.

February 14, 1975	The Santa Catalina Island Conservancy was deeded 88 percent of the island—42,135 acres or sixty-six square miles—from the Wrigley family through the Santa Catalina Island Company.
April 12, 1977	Philip K. Wrigley passed away in Wisconsin.
1978	The island's manual telephone switchboard system was replaced by a computerized system. The first Catalina Marathon was run under the management of Hans Albrecht. The Wrigley Mansion on Mount Ada was donated to the University of Southern California by the Santa Catalina Island Company.
May 29, 1979	The fiftieth anniversary of the opening of the Casino was celebrated in Avalon.
1980	The Institute for Wildlife Studies, in partnership with the Catalina Island Conservancy, reintroduced the bald eagle to the island after the iconic bird's disappearance from the Channel Islands in the 1960s due to DDT poisoning.
November 14, 1980	The *SueJac*, a schooner, ran aground on Casino Point.
November 29, 1981	The body of actress Natalie Wood was recovered near a beached dinghy off Catalina near Two Harbors. Her drowning death has been the subject of speculation and theory ever since.
1983	A fire burned four hundred acres adjacent to Catalina Harbor.
January 30, 1984	Six people were killed when a private Learjet overshot the Airport in the Sky runway and plummeted off a ninety-foot bluff.
1985	The University of Southern California, with the Catalina Island Conservancy and private parties, entered into a thirty-year agreement to operate the Wrigley Mansion as a bed-and-breakfast establishment called the Inn at Mount Ada.

July 30, 1990	The wooden schooner *Diosa del Mar*, or "*Goddess of the Sea*," built in 1898 for the Vanderbilt clan and owned by many others, sank near Ship Rock off the northern West End.
June 25, 1991	Avalon became the first city in California to switch on a reverse osmosis desalination plant, located at Pebbly Beach, powered by diesel generators. During times of drought, the plant can produce some 170,000 gallons of fresh water daily.
February 2, 1994	A retirement dinner aboard the RMS *Queen Mary* in Long Beach was held for A. Douglas and Joanie Propst. Doug Propst was the first president of the Catalina Island Conservancy and had supervised the Santa Catalina Island Company's cattle program from 1953 until his conservancy post in the 1970s.
1998	*Saturday Night Live!* star Phil Hartman was shot to death by his wife, Brynn Hartman, who killed herself hours after the murder. The couple's ashes were scattered in Emerald Bay, as per Hartman's will.
1999	Canine distemper almost wiped out the endemic Catalina Island fox. The recovery effort, through a partnership between the Catalina Island Conservancy and the Institute for Wildlife Studies, saved the species from extinction.
November 1999	After a brief hiatus in its feral goat removal program, the Institute for Wildlife Studies and the Catalina Island Conservancy continued removing the non-native animals, whose overgrazing had destroyed natural habitats.
October 1, 2001	Stephen Otto Reitz woke up in Room 2 at Avalon's Casa Mariquita Hotel and found his married girlfriend, Eva Marie Weinfurtner, on the floor, stabbed and beaten to death. Later, his sleepwalking defense was rejected, and he was convicted of first-degree murder.

2004	After an intensified years-long effort, the last feral goat was removed from Catalina.
December 2004	The Catalina Island Conservancy, in partnership with the Lakota Rosebud Reservation in South Dakota and the Morongo Band of Mission Indians' Tongva descendants, shipped one hundred American bison off Catalina to join the Great Plains herd.
2006	The Nature Center at Avalon Canyon was completed by Los Angeles County for operation by the Catalina Island Conservancy. The fishing trawler *Infidel* sank in 150 feet of water from an overload of squid off southeastern Catalina Island.
May 18, 2006	The body of former Honolulu and Denver disc jockey Steven Bailey Williams was found floating off Catalina. In 2011, a state appeals court upheld the murder conviction of Harvey S. Morrow, a lifelong scam artist, who had shot Williams in the back of the head.
April 2007	A fire accidentally started by a workman burned 4,750 acres and threatened the city of Avalon. A home and two commercial buildings were lost in the blaze. The Institute for Wildlife Studies decided not to intervene by artificially incubating bald eagle eggs off-site from Catalina nests, as it had in past years due to DDT poisoning, which had weakened the shells, causing them to crack under the parents' weights. The birds incubated the eggs and raised the hatchlings on their own on the island for the first time in decades.
May 25, 2008	A tour helicopter crashed near the Banning House at Two Harbors, killing three passengers.

2009	The Catalina Island Conservancy opened the 37.2-mile Trans-Catalina Trail to the public.
	The Catalina Island Conservancy began a successful, leading-edge bison contraception program to keep the island-wide herd close to 150 animals.
January 11, 2009	Four tons of squid net, which had been ensnaring and killing marine life off the East End, was cut away and hauled aboard the *Captain Jack*.
2010	The Santa Catalina Island Company opened the popular zip line experience in Descanso Canyon.
December 2010	The California Fish & Game Commission approved a set of Marine Protected Areas (MPAs) for the waters around Catalina, including Arrow Point to Lion Head Point, Catalina Harbor, Farnsworth Offshore and Onshore areas, Lovers Cove, Casino Point, Long Point, Blue Cavern and Bird Rock.
December 10, 2010	Television director Michael Caffey listed Bird Rock for sale for $875,000. Bird Rock, which is stained white with sea gull guano, sits on the north side of Catalina, about 1,500 feet off the mainland side of Isthmus Cove.

Avalon never seems to lose its quaint charm. The twelve-story-high Casino stands out even from this vantage point. *Photo by Justin Peter.*

2012	After a decade of careful nurturing by the Catalina Island Conservancy and the Institute for Wildlife Studies, more than 1,500 endemic Catalina Island foxes were estimated to exist in the wild in one of America's most successful endangered species recovery efforts.
July 6, 2012	The Los Angeles County Sheriff's Department reopened the Natalie Wood case after determining that some of the bruises on her body were not consistent with drowning. The cause of death was changed from "accidental drowning" to "drowning and other undetermined factors."

GLOSSARY

A

ABALONE POINT: This small cape at the southern hook of Lovers Cove, six hundred yards east of Avalon Bay, divides the bay from Pebbly Beach.

AIRPORT IN THE SKY: Built at Buffalo Springs by leveling two mountaintops, this airfield was opened in 1946 by the Santa Catalina Island Company to serve private and commercial planes. In the past, United Airlines, with which Philip K. Wrigley was involved, flew in and out. Today, the airport is owned and operated by the Catalina Island Conservancy. The hangar at the airport was originally located at Hamilton Cove in Avalon. The Hamilton Cove airport was constructed in 1931 for seaplanes and no longer exists.

AIRPORT LOOP TRAIL: This popular 2.3-mile hiking trail near Airport in the Sky provides spectacular views of the island's interior, including the two highest peaks, Mount Orizaba and Black Jack Mountain. There are also remnants of a soapstone quarry used by the Tongva, the Native Americans who lived on the island. Partial bowls are visible from the trail.

AIRPORT ROAD: These five miles of variably paved roadway connect Middle Ranch Junction and the Airport in the Sky.

ARROW POINT: The northernmost portion of the island is 3.3 miles east of Land's End on the West End, between Parsons' Landing and Emerald Bay.

ART AND ARTISTS: The history of capturing Catalina's beautiful landscapes on canvas goes back to 1860 and developed more fully through the 1930s.

The Airport in the Sky tower was completed after World War II to serve passengers flying United Airlines on regularly scheduled flights to Catalina from Long Beach. *Photo by Justin Peter.*

Outdoor landscape painters used impressionistic techniques to capture subtle colors and textures on canvas. The French term *en plein air* (meaning "in open air") had yet to be coined. As more portable paints (in tubes) and collapsible easels were perfected, artists were able to get out of the studio. As Catalina pioneers such as George Shatto and the Banning brothers promoted Catalina to the mainland, the island became a mecca for American landscape painters. Granville Redmond, Alson Clark, Elmer Wachtel and many others discovered the charms of Catalina and expressed them through their work.

One painter, John Gutzon Borglum (1867–1941), celebrated the Bannings' stagecoach business in *Staging in California*, painted in 1889. The painting was purchased by Hancock Banning and was one of the many important works on display at the Hotel Metropole. The painting and others in that collection were destroyed in the 1915 fire that burned the Metropole to the ground. Borglum went on to gain fame, not as a painter, but as the sculptor of presidential portraits on Mount Rushmore, which he and assistants carved from 1927 until his death in 1941. His son, Lincoln Borglum, finished the monumental work. Later outdoor painters on Catalina included Joe Duncan Gleason and Frank Cuprien, who actually lived in Avalon for about six months. Outdoor painting and impressionism went out of style in the 1930s, giving way to abstract painting and realism. However, many other artists, such as Roger M. "Bud" Upton and Henry Vander Velde carried on the tradition on Catalina by painting the island's scenic wonders, not outdoors but in their studios.

In 1958, the Catalina Art Festival was born—an event that continues today. In 1985, the plein air movement experienced a revival, especially on Catalina. Denise Burns, an artist who moved to Catalina, formed the Plein Air Painters of America (PAPA). In 1996, PAPA morphed into the Society for the Advancement of Plein-Air Painting (SAPAP). The nonprofit organization's purpose was to educate the public in the art of plein-air painting's history and promote its appreciation. In 2011, members of SAPAP created *Catalina: The Wild Side* Art Show & Sale to benefit the Catalina Island Conservancy. Artworks of Catalina's landscapes are displayed in the permanent conservancy collection at the Nature Center in Avalon Canyon.

AUTOS AND AUTOETTES: In 1910, a Model T Ford owned by Allan Hancock was the first to blaze a trail from Avalon to Two Harbors. It was driven by F. Lawrence and carried a party of newspapermen from the *Los Angeles Examiner*. They made the trip in four hours. The second automobile, a Packard owned by Judge J.B. Banning, was brought across the channel on the deck of the SS *Hermosa* and unloaded at Isthmus Cove in 1912. Leaving the Banning home with the good judge at the wheel and Ernest Windel as passenger, the car made the run to Avalon in two hours and ten minutes. By the late 1940s, no more than one hundred cars were on the island. In the late 1930s, residents and visitors could rent pony-pulled wicker-basket coaches that could hold two or three people. By the late 1950s, three-wheeled golf carts were popular to rent. Visitors who flew into the Airport in the Sky could rent two-seat Fiats for the ten-mile drive down to Avalon.

The island's vehicle boom started in the 1960s, when condominiums became a trend and the population expanded. Gas-powered golf carts, or "autoettes," soon crowded the streets. To control the number of autoettes, the Avalon City Council decreed one vehicle and one autoette per residence. Today, 1,600 residential autoettes, 100 commercial autoettes and about 600 automobiles are on the island. However, residents are on a fifteen- to twenty-five-year waiting list to bring additional autos to Catalina. Small vehicles, such as Smart Cars and Mini Coopers, which take up the same amount of space as golf

Pebbly Beach is toured by motor coach. Most automobiles are kept to a minimum on the island, but golf carts and other small cars are most often seen. *Courtesy of Marvin Carlberg.*

carts, don't have waiting times and are capable of driving the roads past Hogsback Gate into the interior.

AVALON: The only city and main population center of Catalina Island has traditionally, in the late twentieth and early twenty-first centuries, had about 3,500 year-round residents and nearly 1 million annual visitors. Michigan real estate speculator George Shatto bought the island for $200,000 in 1887 and created a settlement at what was then Timms Landing on the horseshoe-shaped Bay of the Moons. Augustus Timms operated a warehouse on the California mainland shore where San Pedro exists today and invariably used the locale of the future Avalon for trading with Yankee ships. Shatto's sister-in-law, Etta Whitney, conceived the name Avalon, which was taken from Alfred Lord Tennyson's poem "Idylls of the King" about a legendary isle where King Arthur healed his battle wounds.

AVALON BAY: Called "Bay of Moons" by the native Tongva, this curved bay was the most populous part of the island when Spanish explorers discovered Santa Catalina Island, which they named "San Salvador," in 1542. It was renamed Santa Catalina sixty years later by Sebastián Vizcaíno after his ship arrived on the eve of the feast day of Saint Catherine of Alexandria.

Private homes are depicted on the east side of Avalon. Note the newly refurbished Holly Hill House on the far left. *Photo by Justin Peter.*

A view of Avalon is seen through a very busy Avalon Harbor. On any given day, the craft in or just outside Avalon Harbor range from giant cruise vessels and Catalina Express passenger boats to lavish yachts and commercial fishing trawlers to dinghies and rowboats. *Photo by Justin Peter.*

AVALON CANYON: The canyon that rises in a southwestern direction from Avalon Bay up toward East Peak contains the Nature Center at Avalon Canyon, Catalina Island Golf Course and the Wrigley Memorial & Botanic Garden—all connected by Avalon Canyon Road.

AVALON CEMETERY: Located up Avalon Canyon from downtown Avalon, Cemetery Road cuts off of Country Club Drive above Avalon School. Cemetery Road leads to the final resting place of several Catalina pioneers and former residents. When Nathaniel Parsons (b. August 24, 1811, in Gloucester, Massachusetts) died on August 22, 1889, he requested to be buried in Avalon. He was one of the twins whose surname identified Parsons' Landing and was resident Captain Alonzo Wheeler's uncle. It was Catalina's third death in the Shatto resort era and the first with the expressed pre-death wish to be buried in Avalon. No cemetery existed. So Mrs. Sophia Wheeler, Ed Whitney and Harry Polley trekked up Avalon Canyon and found a spot they deemed suitable. Aside from Captain "Nat" Parsons, others buried in the Avalon Cemetery include boat designer Al Bombard and notable Avalon roustabout "Chicken Johnnie" Brinkley, as well as film and television comedian Winstead Sheffield "Doodles" Weaver, the brother of former NBC TV executive Sylvester "Pat" Weaver and uncle of actress Sigourney Weaver—among more than one thousand other souls.

This view overlooks Avalon from the vantage point of the hills to the east of town. The image is from the early 1900s. *Courtesy of Marvin Carlberg.*

AVALON CITY GOVERNMENT: When the Banning Brothers took over the island in 1892, they kept the non-alcohol policy adopted by George Shatto before them. Business boomed in Avalon despite it being a resort with a "dry" status. In 1894, the Bannings established the Santa Catalina Island Company to provide residents with dependable electricity, gas and water barged from the mainland—at little or no costs to recipients. This arrangement ended in 1909, when the residents, acting as the Freeholders Improvement Association, took the Island Company to court over the parallel pier extending three hundred feet out into Avalon Harbor. With this pier, the Island Company controlled all harbor commerce. The Freeholders won the suit, using the planks of the parallel pier to build the municipal Pleasure Pier, which they eventually purchased from the Island Company for five dollars.

The Island Company called the Freeholder's bluff: "If that is the way you want it, why don't you become 'incorporated' and then you can pay all of the expenses and experience all of the headaches that we have kept from you all these years!" On June 19, 1913, the town voted 132 to 82

In 1904, the Banning brothers built a large outdoor amphitheater (foreground), often referred to as the Avalon Bowl. The amphitheater was located on the south end of Avalon and could seat several hundred people. Some bands would perform concerts at the amphitheater and then play again at the dance pavilion, completed in 1892. The dance pavilion was on the site of the present-day Pavilion Hotel on Crescent Avenue. The amphitheater was torn down in 1931. *Courtesy of Marvin Carlberg.*

Avalon Harbor around the turn of the twentieth century, during the Banning years. Notice the spire of the dance pavilion near the center of the photo and the Holly Hill House on the left. *Courtesy of Marvin Carlberg.*

for incorporation as a "sixth-class city" (population 999 or fewer). The new city immediately granted licenses to three businesses to sell alcoholic beverages. It also asked Avalon's citizenry to vote on a $125,000 bond for a water works, gas and electric plants, a sewer system and the new pleasure pier. The citizens voted down the bond issue, leaving the Island Company to continue administering utilities.

AVIATION: On May 10, 1912, aviation pioneer Glenn L. Martin flew an amphibious aircraft of his own design from Newport Beach to Avalon. The story is that Glenn's mother came to wish him well in his endeavor. He was wearing dusty work clothes. She insisted that he go home and change into something more appropriate for the occasion. While he was gone, she sewed a piece of the cloth wing that had ripped loose. She later flew with her son in support of his work, a demonstration of the potential of flying. The thirty-three-mile-long flight to Avalon lasted thirty-seven minutes, with an average speed of less than fifty-five miles per hour.

Commercial air transportation literally took off on July 12, 1919, when Sydney Chaplin, the half-brother of film legend Charlie Chaplin, started Chaplin Airlines. With pilot A.C. Burns, Chaplin Airlines began regular flights to the mainland in a three-passenger Curtiss biplane equipped with floats. The costly service was discontinued after two months, but Burns stayed with the plane, offering scenic flights at five dollars apiece. Throughout the 1920s, Pacific Marine Airways of Wilmington attempted scheduled service to Avalon, but profits were elusive. In 1928, Pacific Marine was absorbed by Western Air Express, which operated a few twin-engine Sikorskys into Avalon for three years. When Western Air Express folded in 1930, P.K. Wrigley started the Wilmington–Catalina Airline, offering daily service at Hamilton Cove.

The first landing strip on Catalina was on a specially graded road near El Rancho Escondido in 1938. The first plane to land was a twin-engine Lockheed Lodestar piloted by William Patterson of United Airlines and Justin Dart, founder of the Owl-Rexall Drug Company. Wrigley leveled two mountain peaks and filled in three canyons to create the runway for Airport in the Sky, which was stalled temporarily in December 1941 by World War II and then completed and opened in 1946. United Airlines, for which Wrigley was a board member, made regularly scheduled passenger trips to the island from Long Beach. Commercial landings ended in 1954. In October 1959, forty private planes landed at the airport. In 1953, Avalon Air Transport continued seaplane access to Catalina until it ceased operation in 1968.

Philip Knight Wrigley started the Wilmington–Catalina Airline in 1930 at Hamilton Cove's Catalina Airport. The turntable allowed seaplanes to land and reposition for takeoff within minutes. *Courtesy of Marvin Carlberg.*

B

BALLAST POINT: Ballast Point is on the east side of the eight-hundred-yard-wide entrance to Catalina Harbor. It's the site of the oldest shipwreck known on the island, that of *Ning Po*, the 1753 vintage Chinese smuggling ship. Ballast Point Road is the short dirt road from Two Harbors southwest to Ballast Point.

BANNING, CAPTAIN HANCOCK: Hancock (May 12, 1865–August 7, 1925) was the youngest of the three sons of Phineas Banning who survived to adulthood. With his two brothers and two sisters, Hancock purchased Catalina Island from George Shatto in 1892. Hancock served as vice-president of the Santa Catalina Island Company and is credited with many of the developments that led to the sale of the island to Wrigley as a resort.

The three brothers had very different and distinct personalities. Historian John Steven McGroarty described Hancock as "a man of progressive outlook and his far-ranging vision was responsive to the needs of the American public; and the public spirited in meeting the obligations of his position." Hancock was also said to have a sense of humor. One story reported that Hancock was returning from Middle Ranch on a stagecoach to catch the 3:15 p.m. steamer back to the mainland. His close friend, Captain Smith of the SS *Cabrillo*, had already directed the ship to leave dock fifty feet from the hurrying Hancock. "Hey, come back here, you big Scotchman! I want to go over!" Banning yelled. Captain Smith stood silent and then said, "There's too much current! You set the time, 3:15, for this boat to leave. There's another boat tomorrow!" Banning shouted, "You're fired!" Smith replied, "Sure, I'll take a drink with you tomorrow!" In the retelling of this account, he did.

Banning was someone who saw the glass as always half full. According to a story told by the secretary of the Banning Company, Dave P. Fleming, the Bannings were in a prolonged suit with the City of Los Angeles over the title to the tidelands adjacent to the harbor in San Pedro. Finally, one Sunday morning, Hancock received a message from Washington saying that the United States Supreme Court had decided the case in favor of the city. Hancock looked up and cheerfully remarked, "Just got some good news. We won't have to pay taxes on that tideland anymore."

BANNING, CAPTAIN WILLIAM: William (1857–1946) was the eldest of the three sons of Phineas Banning to survive to adulthood. Along with his two brothers and two sisters, he owned Santa Catalina Island from 1892 until 1919.

The home of Captain Hancock Banning in Descanso Canyon, circa 1910. Banning, with his brothers William and Joseph Brent (J.B.), owned the island from 1891 to 1919. *Courtesy of Marvin Carlberg.*

William followed in his father's footsteps as a stagecoach driver. Phineas drove a coach regularly in his younger years between the settlements of Los Angeles and San Pedro. William earned the reputation as the finest amateur six-in-hand coach driver in the West. He reportedly could drive a team down from Catalina's East Summit to Avalon in eighteen minutes, about the same amount of time it takes to drive a vehicle down the road today. Later in life, William co-authored, with his nephew George Hugh Banning, *Six Horses*, a history of U.S. overland stagecoach lines from 1857 to 1867.

William's take-charge approach to stagecoaches carried over to his business acumen. In 1908, with William as president, the Santa Catalina Island Company became embroiled in an argument with the California Naval Militia in the so-called Avalon Incident, in which uninvited sailors off the USS *Alert* showed up for a Fourth of July party in Avalon. The sailors were unceremoniously dismissed. "Drunk and disorderly" was the description given by F.H. Lowe, the manager of the pavilion where the party was held. This accusation was vehemently denied by Lieutenant Commander George M. Bauer of the *Alert*. Banning's influence was felt when the adjutant general and then California governor James Gillett advised the navy that no "National Guard or Naval Militia of this State would be permitted to

This wild ride down Stage Road was in 1899. At the reins was Captain William Banning, considered the finest amateur six-in-hand driver in the West. The Bannings kept their coaches in operation until 1914. That year, the widening of the road brought automobiles into use on the island. *Courtesy of Marvin Carlberg.*

land on Santa Catalina Island while under the then existing ownership and management, except for purely necessary military purposes."

In 1896, the Bannings formed and deeded the island to the Santa Catalina Island Company. In the beginning, the Bannings leased only land; this resulted in poorly constructed and maintained buildings. In 1906, they lessened up on their leasing policy, and nine hundred lots were offered for sale at starting prices of $1,500 for view sites. Peter Gano acquired his lot for the Holly Hill House for $500. When William Wrigley Jr. purchased controlling interest of the Santa Catalina Island Company, he retained Captain William Banning as vice-president.

BANNING, GENERAL PHINEAS: Phineas (August 19, 1830–March 8, 1885) was known as the "Father of the Port of Los Angeles" or "Father of LA Harbor." He casually speculated in exploiting Santa Catalina as a resort. Phineas would arrange sumptuous champagne boat excursions from his wharf at San Pedro to see Catalina. These adventures instilled in his three sons and two daughters a love for the island that led them to purchase it from George R. Shatto a few years after Phineas's death. Phineas made a name for himself first as a stagecoach driver and later as a Los Angeles business owner. Most of his wealth was acquired through the freight and cargo industry, but he was also instrumental in starting a lucrative telegraph communication system from Los Angeles to San Francisco. He was elected to the California state senate from 1865 to 1868 and helped ratify the Thirteenth Amendment abolishing slavery. He acquired the honorary title of brigadier general of the California First Brigade during the Civil War when he ceded land to the Union army for a fort to be built at Wilmington. From that time forward, he insisted on being called General Phineas Banning.

In 1870, Banning married Mary Hollister (1846–1919), a wealthy heiress whose family lent their name to the city of Hollister, California. In this second marriage for Phineas, he and Mary had three children, two of whom survived to adulthood—Mary Hollister Banning (1871–1953) and Lucy Tichenor Banning (1873–1929), whose tales of love lost make for interesting reading even today.

BANNING, JUDGE JOSEPH BRENT (1862–1920): Known to his family and friends as "J.B.," Joseph was the middle of the three Banning brothers who operated island concerns before selling Catalina to William Wrigley Jr. J.B. gave his attention to the Isthmus while his brothers focused on Avalon. He spent much of his time in the summer home built by the Banning brothers at the Isthmus. That manse today is a bed-and-breakfast known as the Banning House Lodge. Banning House Road is an approximately two-mile stretch of the Trans-Catalina Trail heading northwest to the Banning House, overlooking Two Harbors.

BEACON STREET: This Avalon street was named by city developer George Shatto after his favorite street in Boston.

BEN WESTON BEACH: Sheep farmer Nathaniel Andrew Narbonne, whose surname adorns a long north–south avenue through Los Angeles County, as well as a high school in Harbor City, partnered with a Lomita-area farmer named Ben Weston to grow wheat and raise sheep on Catalina in the late 1800s. Ben Weston Canyon Trail is a mile-and-a-half hiking trail from Middle Ranch Road down through the watershed to the beach. Nearby Ben Weston Point is accessible by a service road from Middle Ranch Road just north of Ben Weston Beach, aka Mills Landing. The point formerly was the site of a World War II–era bunker containing a long-range shore gun.

BIG FISHERMAN'S COVE: This inlet just northeast of Isthmus Cove at Two Harbors is the home of the Wrigley Marine Science Center operated by the University of Southern California.

BIG GEIGER/LITTLE GEIGER COVES: Located on the northwest side of Catalina, the big cove is west of the Isthmus and just east of Howland's Landing. There are no moorings, but it is reported to be one of the best natural anchorages on the island. Big and Little Geiger Coves are named

Ben Weston Beach on the windward side of the island near Little Harbor was the home of early island squatter Ben Weston, who built a stone house for himself at the beach. Today, it's a popular surfing beach. *Photo by Justin Peter.*

for George L. Geiger, who attended the Boy Scout Camp at Emerald Bay in the late 1920s and then built an eighteen-foot gaff-rigged yawl, the *Daisy R. George.* George and Thelma Geiger had six children and would summer annually aboard the *Daisy R* until 1967, when George launched the twenty-six-foot sloop *Thelma.* George died in 1992, and Thelma followed in 2006.

BIG SPRINGS CANYON: This watershed drains down to Little Harbor on the windward side of the island. Big Springs Reservoir, a man-made pond, is located just off Big Springs Road, a dirt hiking road that connects with Little Harbor Road a little less than two miles north of Little Harbor. Big Springs Road ends at Empire Landing.

BINNACLE ROCK: This offshore landmark is west-northwest of the similar and adjacent Church Rock, near the East End, at the southernmost point of the island.

BIRD PARK: Once the world's largest aviary with eight thousand birds in more than five hundred cages on eight acres in Avalon Canyon, this colorful and loud zoological garden was one of Catalina's great attractions, beginning in 1928. William Wrigley Jr. and British gamekeeper E.H. Lewis pooled

William Wrigley Jr. created the Bird Park in Avalon Canyon in 1928. The eight-acre park featured an octagonal building that was the former Sugarloaf Casino, completed in 1920. When the much larger Casino was built in 1929, the smaller building was dismantled and set up in Avalon Canyon. Five hundred separate cages displayed eight thousand exotic birds from around the world. Following World War II, the Bird Park was scaled back and never regained its prewar popularity. It closed in 1966. *Courtesy of Marvin Carlberg.*

The entrance to the Bird Park was along Avalon Canyon Road. Delivering tourists to the popular attraction is an early Santa Catalina Island Company tour bus. *Courtesy of Marvin Carlberg.*

ideas with the former's investment of $250,000 to realize the park, which contained macaws and toucans, ibises and ostriches, cockatoos and hornbills—species from all corners of the globe. One mynah named Jimmie was prone to screeds of squawk, after which he would suddenly clam up for a beat and then scream, "Quiet!" The park was scaled back during World War II and never regained its 1930s' popularity. It closed in 1966, and the birds were transferred to the Los Angeles Zoo and elsewhere.

BIRD ROCK: About 500 yards off the eastern shore of Two Harbors, Bird Rock reaches a height of thirty-seven feet above sea level and is about 150 yards in length. It's a roosting place for thousands of gulls, cormorants and pelicans. As a result, the rock is nearly white with bird droppings. In 1894, the Banning brothers built a cabin on the rock for the purpose of establishing homestead rights. It burned down. Helen K. Morton Webb bought the rock in 1930 with acreage from Valentine's script, which deserves a brief explanation. Don Manuel Micheltosena, governor of Mexico's Alta California in 1844, granted 13,300 acres to Don Juan Miranda. After the United States took over California, attorney Thomas B. Valentine succeeded in having Don Miranda reimbursed for his lost acreage through the issuance of "Valentine's script," good for equal acreage of unappropriated lands. Mrs. Morton later tried unsuccessfully to sell Bird Rock to William Wrigley Jr. for $100,000. The last known owner of the 1.3-acre island was filmmaker Michael Caffey, father of Go-Go's band member Charlotte Caffey.

BIRDS: America's symbol is also Catalina Island's most iconic avian species. The American bald eagle was reestablished on Catalina in 1980 through the work of the Institute for Wildlife Studies (IWS) with the Catalina Island Conservancy. DDT poisoning had decimated the big birds. The since-outlawed pollutant, absorbed by the birds' major prey—fish—was ingested by the eagles and created weak shells on the eggs that they laid. The shells cracked under the adults' weight during incubation. Eagles laid eggs in Catalina nests after the species reintroduction, but the shells broke before hatching because DDT was still present. The scientists retrieved eggs, hatched them in off-site incubators and returned the chicks to the nests. The parents accepted them and raised them. In 2007, IWS scientists allowed two nesting pairs to lay eggs and attempt to hatch young naturally. DDT levels had finally decreased enough to allow bald eagles to successfully hatch eggs in the wild. A dozen other birds of prey inhabit the island, including peregrine falcons, Cooper's hawks, red-tailed hawks and American kestrels.

Bird Rock is so named because of the thousands of birds that have claimed the rock and painted it white with their guano over the centuries. It is a 1.3-acre piece of land 1,500 feet off the mainland side of Isthmus Cove. Helen K. Morton Webb tried unsuccessfully to sell Bird Rock to William Wrigley Jr. for $100,000. *Photo by Justin Peter.*

A wide gamut of West Coast seabirds thrives here, including brown pelicans and cormorants, as well as the rare and enigmatic Scripps's murrelet. The island's freshwater ponds, particularly Thompson Reservoir, serve as sojourns on the Pacific Flyway for teal, ruddy ducks and others. Ravens and crows are omnipresent residents. A conspicuous resident is the loud, redheaded and resourceful acorn woodpecker.

BLACKBUCK ANTELOPE: Sightings of the elusive blackbuck antelope continue. A popular viewing site is the patio of the DC-3 Gifts & Grill at the Airport in the Sky. The island presence of the big ungulates is traced to the Santa Catalina Island Company's attempt in the 1970s to turn the island into a "big game" retreat. One male and two females were introduced. However, because the animals were indigenous to India, the species never caught on and populated the island like the mule deer, which were brought to the island by the State of Catalina in the 1920s and 1930s for hunting purposes.

BLACK JACK MOUNTAIN: The second highest point on Catalina, at 2,010 feet, and the only one after the 2,097-foot-high Mount Orizaba that is more than 2,000 feet above sea level, this pinnacle features access via Black

Jack Gate to Black Jack Campground near the former Black Jack Mine. In 1923, David Malcolm Renton, under the direction of William Wrigley Jr., opened a mine here. In a mere nine months, some three thousand tons of minerals priced at $90,000 were extracted and shipped out. The zinc and silver were separated from the ore with the use of saltwater flotation rather than oil at a mill in operation at White's Landing. Aerial cable tramways conveyed the ore from the mine to the mill. Evidence of the mining activity is still present in the landscape.

BLACK POINT: This is an isolated stretch of rocky coastline on the northern side of the island near the West End. The neighboring rocky beach to the west is Starlight Beach, the official beginning or end of the Trans-Catalina Trail.

BLUE CAVERN POINT: Located just east of the Isthmus, Blue Cavern Point contains many caves that are accessible, depending on the tides, to scuba divers and kayakers.

BOMBARD, ALFRED: Miss Catalina speedboats were designed and built by one of Catalina's most avid and admired watermen. Bombard struck up a friendship and then a partnership with Wilbur White, Edgar Dearden and Jack Roth. Together, these men started Catalina Speed Boat Company on February 8, 1922. Alfred designed the company's V-bottom speedboats, which were twenty-nine feet, eleven inches long and powered by a single, direct-drive Liberty V-12 gasoline engine of the type used by U.S. Navy seaplanes during World War I. For most tourists, the most memorable aspect of the Miss Catalina speedboats was the tradition of loading a boat with people, including as many pretty girls as possible, and zooming out of Avalon Bay to meet the incoming steamer fifteen minutes before it docked. The speedboat would circle the steamer a number of times, skimming along, barely touching the waves. Those on both vessels waved and smiled—and it was an excellent advertisement for speedboat rides. Alfred's son, Doug Bombard, with his knowledge of Catalina's currents and tides, found Natalie Wood's body in 1981.

BOSKEY DELL: Boskey Dell is an idyllic picnic spot in Cottonwood Canyon, where William Wrigley Jr. built a stone barbecue and a covered eating area. Frequent guests were the Chicago Cubs, owned by Wrigley, who hosted the team's annual spring training rite on the island from 1921 to 1952. The name is taken from Homer's *Odyssey* and translates as a "sheltered place."

BOUCHETTE, SANTOS: Santos Louis "William" Bouchette was the son of Louis Bouchette, a shipmate of Samuel Prentiss on the brigantine *Danube*, the first ship to wreck on the rocks at San Pedro in 1824 (often referenced as 1828). Santos used the names "William" or "Louis" when it suited him and spelled his last name "Bochard" or "Boshard" at times. An article printed in the *Catalina Islander* in July 1931 reported that a Louis Bouchette (supposedly of the *Danube* but most likely Santos himself) was thought to also be the same man who operated the "Bouchette Mines, at Cherry Valley, Parson's Beach, and Johnsons (now Emerald Bay), from 1860 to 1876." He incorporated his business under the name of Mineral Hills Mine.

Before dying, Prentiss told Santos Bouchette of the hidden treasure buried under a tree on Catalina. As the story goes, the confident Santos began cutting down trees supposedly for firewood—but he was actually looking for the hidden treasure. For him, the real treasure ended up being a "silver lode" in Cherry Valley, or so he told potential investors in Los Angeles, brandishing samples. Andrew Joughin advanced Bouchette several thousand dollars in 1860. All was well, until early one morning in 1876, when he loaded a small boat with silver ore and, with his wife seated in the bow, headed toward San Pedro for provisions. He never arrived. One story suggests that he made it to lower California and, after disposing of his silver, gave his wife money to go back to France. She was later heard of in Paris. The remaining gold, silver and ore of Catalina were left for David Malcolm Renton to uncover in 1923. Those who advanced Santos money never recovered their investments. (Bouchette should also not be confused with Stephen Boucher, who later legally changed his last name to Boushey and for whom a canyon on Catalina is named.)

BOUSHEY CANYON ROAD: A very steep hiking trail a bit more than a mile in length on the West End connects Silver Peak and West Roads between Parson's Landing and Emerald Bay. The road is named for Stephen Boushey, formerly Boucher or Boushay and spelled many ways, who, sometime after 1866, came to Catalina with two partners and mined for lead and silver. In 1881, Boushay left for Kern County in California, where he located antimony mines in the San Emigdio Mountains.

BUFFALO SPRINGS RESERVOIR: This small pond west of the runway at the Airport in the Sky is along Airport Loop Trail. It's a favorite watering hole for the island's bison herd.

BULLRUSH CANYON: This watershed on the southeast portion of the East End is accessible via the three-mile-plus dirt hiking road known as Bullrush Canyon Road, which connects Valley of the Moons with Thompson Reservoir. Bullrush Reservoir is a small reservoir along the road.

BUTTONSHELL BEACH: Flanked by Hen Rock on the leeward side of the East End, this is believed to be the beach from which Native Americans gathered shells for barter. Buttonlike shells are abundant.

C

CABRILLO, JUAN RODRIGUEZ: Cabrillo (March 13, 1499–January 3, 1543) was a Portuguese explorer who landed on the island in October 1542 and named it San Salvador. His name appears in the ranks of those who served in the army of conquistador Hernan Cortes, about 1519, and he joined in the conquest of Mexico and Guatemala. Cabrillo died on San Miguel Island in the Northern Channel Islands. It was reported that he died from complications of a broken leg incurred from a fall during a brief skirmish with Native Americans. It is thought that he may have been buried on Catalina Island.

CABRILLO BEACH: Located to the east of Gibraltar Beach, this long, sandy beach was used by the Boy Scouts of America for years. The beach here is mostly cobblestone, with more sand toward the water's edge. Cabrillo is one of the island's favorite snorkeling spots and a boat-in campsite.

CABRILLO MOLE: Visitors who arrive in Avalon aboard the larger Catalina Express catamarans will tie up at the Cabrillo Mole. The mole was built in the mid-1960s on the south side of Avalon Bay to replace the dismantled steamer pier. The mole is also a popular fishing spot for anglers.

CACTUS PEAK: The highest point on the Salta Verde Ridge across Catalina's remote southern coastline, this peak rises 1,560 feet above sea level from China Point, more than a mile to the southwest.

CALIFORNIA CHANNEL ISLANDS: Catalina Island's home archipelago is located off the Southern California coast, including Santa Cruz, San Miguel, Santa Rosa and Anacapa in the northern group and Catalina, San Clemente, Santa Barbara and San Nicholas in the southern group. Catalina is the largest of the southern Channel Islands and the only privately owned isle of the whole group. It is also the most visited, receiving nearly one million tourists and other visitors each year. Most of the northern Channel Islands form Channel Islands National Park.

CAPE CANYON: This canyon in the island's interior is located south of Mount Black Jack and east of Mount Orizaba. Cape Canyon Road and Cape Canyon Reservoir are located within its confines.

The then new Casino building is seen from Descanso Beach, where the Bannings built the Hotel St. Catherine. *Courtesy of Marvin Carlberg.*

CAPE CORTEZ: The western arc of Lobster Bay, below Mount Torquemada on the southern coast of the West End, ceases at this land hook.

CASINO POINT: The northern arc of Avalon Bay ends at this mini cape, on which is situated the island's most prominent architectural landmark: the Catalina Island Casino.

CATALINA EXPRESS: The origins of the Catalina Express go back to 1981, when Doug Bombard, who headed the Santa Catalina Island Company's hunting program out of Two Harbors, needed a fast, easy way to get hunters to and from the Isthmus. Up until then, Bombard had used amphibious seaplanes to ferry groups of hunters across the channel. He found that leasing a boat large enough to carry hunters and their equipment wasn't economically feasible. Partnering with his son, Greg, and longtime colleague Tom Rutter, Bombard purchased a sixty-foot boat manufactured in Washington and redesigned it to suit the team's purposes. Today, the fleet consists of eight high-speed vessels, including four catamarans. The largest vessel in operation, the *Catalina Jet*, has the capacity to carry nearly five hundred passengers across the channel. Catalina Express offers year-round service and up to thirty departures daily from Long Beach, San Pedro and Dana Point.

Playful dolphins charm Catalina Express passengers on the way to Avalon. Whales are occasionally sighted on the trip over, and the bigger sea life in Catalina's waters include giant black sea bass, squid, octopus and a variety of sharks. *Photo by Justin Peter.*

CATALINA FLYER: The *Catalina Flyer* is a five-hundred-passenger catamaran ferry operated by Catalina Passenger Service. It has provided daily service since 1988 from the Balboa Pavilion in Newport Beach to the city of Avalon. Prior to 1988, the same run was served by the *Island Holiday* from the mid-1950s until 1978 and the *Catalina Holiday* from 1978 until 1988. Both were also operated by Catalina Passenger Service. The *Catalina Flyer* is the largest passenger-carrying catamaran on the West Coast and, at the time it was launched, was the largest in North America. It makes one round trip daily, leaving Newport Beach for Avalon in the morning and returning from Avalon to Newport Beach in the early evening. A one-way trip takes approximately seventy-five minutes. In a historical footnote, one of the first flying fish excursion boats to operate out of Avalon—in 1911—was called the *Catalina Flyer*.

CATALINA HARBOR: Catalina is nearly two completely different islands joined together by a short stretch of land called the Isthmus. It's not quite a half-mile walk from Two Harbors to Catalina Harbor (or, simply, Cat Harbor) on the windward side of the island. Here is located one of only three remaining buildings from the Civil War in California. The Isthmus

Cat Head marks the entryway to Catalina Harbor on the windward side of the island at the isthmus. Catalina Harbor is called the largest safe harbor between San Diego and San Francisco. *Photo by Justin Peter.*

Barracks was built in 1864 and today is used by the Isthmus Yacht Club. It is also here at Cat Harbor that the Chinese junk *Ning Po*, built in 1753, was moored in its later years. It caught fire by accident during a film shoot in 1938.

CATALINA ISLAND CASINO: Casino Point, where the iconic twelve-story-high Casino has stood for the better part of a century, was formerly Sugarloaf Point. In the 1920s, this premium waterfront site was flattened to make way for the Hotel St. Catherine. Plans changed, and the luxury hotel was built around the point in Descanso Canyon. When William Wrigley Jr. took control of the Santa Catalina Island Company, he supervised the erection of a dance hall, named Sugarloaf Casino, on the spot. This ballroom doubled as Avalon's first high school. Population growth required a bigger building, and Sugarloaf Casino, along with the giant boulder, Sugarloaf Rock, dividing the point from Descanso Bay, was eliminated to build a bigger casino. Approximately $2 million later, on May 29, 1929, the new Casino was finished. Wrigley and David M. Renton supervised the construction from Sumner A. Spaulding and Walter Weber's design. The combination Art Deco and Mediterranean design contained acoustics to

Dancers pack the Avalon Casino Ballroom during the big band era in the 1940s. Many of the great big bands played the Casino, which was also a favorite radio broadcasting spot, including for the popular *Kay Kyser's Kollege of Musical Knowledge. Courtesy of Marvin Carlberg.*

accommodate sound motion pictures: the world's first public sound movie theater. It was the first completely circular big building built in modern times and received the Honor Award from the California Chapter of the American Institute of Architects as "one of the outstanding architectural accomplishments." Also called Catalina Casino and, simply, the Casino, it has dominated most photos of Avalon Bay.

CATALINA ISLAND CONSERVANCY: The Wrigley and Offield families established the Santa Catalina Island Conservancy in 1972 to preserve and restore Catalina Island's natural history. Helen and Philip K. Wrigley and Mrs. Dorothy Wrigley Offield then deeded 42,135 acres from the Santa Catalina Island Company to the conservancy on February 15, 1975, in the final step to ensure that most of the island's wild lands and wildlife would be protected in perpetuity. With this gift, 88 percent of Catalina's interior and more than sixty miles of its coastline were permanently placed under the stewardship of the nonprofit organization. The protection went hand-in-hand with recreational and educational uses, which were reaffirmed in 1974, when the Santa Catalina Island Company signed a fifty-year open-space agreement with Los Angeles County. This agreement guaranteed the public's use of 41,000 acres of the island, which was consistent with established good land conservation practices while providing recreation opportunities. The 1972 articles of incorporation stipulated that the conservancy preserve native plants and animals, biotic communities and geological and geographical formations of educational interest, as well as open-space lands used solely for the enjoyment of scenic beauty. The conservancy was also charged with promoting the study of ecology, including terrestrial and aquatic, natural history, archaeology and conservation, and the ecologically sound and appropriate recreational and educational use of the property by the general public, scientists and others. The conservancy, in partnership with the Institute for Wildlife Studies, eliminated destructive feral livestock and went on to achieve such ecological triumphs as reestablishing the bald eagle on the island and bringing the Catalina Island fox back from the brink of extinction. The conservancy has also taken the lead in eradicating invasive plants on the island and habitat restoration.

CATALINA ISLAND MARINE INSTITUTE (CIMI): A nonprofit educational program run by Guided Discoveries, CIMI is the host to approximately fifteen thousand students a year from school-organized trips and summer camps. Students at CIMI learn marine biology through activities such as snorkeling, hiking and squid dissections. CIMI operates out of three

The Catalina Island Marine Institute (CIMI) manages the summer camp here at Fox Landing. In a year, nearly 100,000 youth stay at one of the several camps on Catalina Island. For many, it's one of their most passionately remembered experiences on the island. *Photo by Justin Peter.*

facilities in Catalina coves: Toyon Bay, a private beach three miles northwest of Avalon; Fox Landing; and Cherry Cove. CIMI operates a 156-foot-tall ship, the *Tole Mour*, which moors at Long Beach's Rainbow Harbor and sails throughout the Channel Islands.

CATALINA ISLAND MUSEUM: Located in the historic Casino building is the keeper of the island's cultural heritage. The museum contains collections numbering more than 100,000 items from seven thousand years of Native American history, more than ten thousand photographs and images, a large collection of Catalina-made pottery and tile, ship models and other artifacts. The museum features exhibits, a gift store and programs, including walking tours of Avalon, classes for students, gallery docents, lectures, an annual film benefit and more. In 2013, the museum began building a larger facility on Metropole Avenue in Avalon.

CHERRY COVE: Located half a mile west of Isthmus Cove, Cherry Cove has ninety-nine moorings. On shore, there is a Boy Scout camp that's been operating since the 1920s. Up in the nearby canyon are large groves of Catalina cherry trees and ironwoods. Catalina Island Marine Institute runs programs here several months each year. A point of land, called Lion's Head, protects this cove from the afternoon winds.

CHERRY VALLEY: In 1830, Captain George Yount found the first gold in California here, nearly two decades ahead of the historically well-known strike at Sutter's Mill. Cherry Valley became the scene of frenzied mining activities during 1864. A dense grove of wild cherry trees grows in the canyon, which opens up onto the beach.

CHICAGO CUBS: William Wrigley Jr. became the majority owner of the National League baseball club in 1921, and the Wrigley family was involved with the team until 1981, when it sold the "lovable losers" to the Tribune Company, owner of the *Chicago Tribune* and other media. The team conducted spring training on Catalina from 1921 through 1951 and helped bring sporting-world attention to the island. The players stayed at the luxurious Hotel St. Catherine on Descanso Bay and played in the ballpark Wrigley built in Avalon Canyon. Such stars as Hack Wilson, Gabby Hartnett, Dizzy Dean and Rogers Hornsby became familiar faces each year in Avalon. A Tampico, Illinois–born baseball broadcaster named Ronald Reagan joined the club in the 1930s and was recruited as an actor on the island by Warner Bros. The island life never seemed to truly benefit the club's fortunes, as the Cubs' last World Series appearance was in 1908.

CHIMES TOWER: This public clock, situated off Chimes Tower Road and above Casino Way, was a gift to the people of Avalon from Ada Wrigley.

The Chimes Tower tolls on the quarter hour between 8:00 a.m. and 8:00 p.m. Hogsback Loop is a popular walk that provides a great view of the Chimes Tower and Avalon Bay. *Photo by Justin Peter.*

The chimes have been tolling on the quarter hour between 8:00 a.m. and 8:00 p.m. since 1925. A stone's throw from the Zane Grey Pueblo Hotel, the building that used to be the author's home, the chimes inspired the never-proven urban legend that Mrs. Wrigley installed them just to annoy the writer's wife.

CHINA POINT: A popular diving location, this point is 7.2 miles west of Church Rock on the southeast side of the island. Its name came from its use by smugglers of illegal Chinese immigrants into California.

CHURCHES: Two years after George Shatto gained control of Catalina Island in 1887, George and Clara Shatto approached the Reverend Charles Spencer Uzzell of the First Congregational Church of Los Angeles to build and maintain a church on Catalina. Uzzell accepted the challenge, and the first church was built in Avalon in 1889. This was the Congregational Church, known today as the Avalon Community Church. The first Roman Catholic house of worship, St. Catherine of Alexandria, located on Beacon Street, was founded in 1900 and is affiliated with the Archdiocese of Los Angeles. The Catalina Bible Church was founded in 1964.

CHURCH ROCK: Off the remote southeastern portion of the East End, approachable by boat only, this rocky outcropping has a steeple-like aspect on one side. It's a favorite haunt of gulls, pelicans and other seabirds.

CIVIL WAR: The westernmost Civil War site in America doubles as the Isthmus Yacht Club (IYC). The IYC is housed in the oldest structure still standing on Catalina. This long house, one of the most conspicuous buildings at Two Harbors, was the Union army barracks built after Company C of the Fourth California Infantry, dispatched from the Union's Southwest headquarters at Camp Drum in Wilmington, surveyed and occupied the island in 1863. The soldiers brought with them camels that were being used experimentally instead of horses. The island was evacuated, except for some miners and shepherds. The military intent was for the island to be a possible penal colony for Union traitors or a Native American reservation. The Union abandoned the barracks and the island in September 1864.

CLARISSA AVENUE: Clarissa was the nickname of Avalon developer George Shatto's wife, Clara "Clarissa" Ruth Alward Whitney Shatto.

COFFEE POT CANYON: This barren canyon suffers from erosion just south of the Valley of the Moons on the island's windward side.

COTTONWOOD BEACH: Just south of Little and Shark Harbors and located along Cape Canyon Road just before it becomes El Rancho Escondido Road, this beach is secluded. Seasonal waters create Cottonwood Creek through the watershed. Cottonwood Canyon offers one of the island's most unique landscapes: a small waterfall during the rainy season. Hikers can reach Cottonwood Beach along the Trans-Catalina Trail. Cottonwood Overlook is the site of the Cottonwood Beach trailhead. Cottonwood Road is a five-mile dirt hiking trail that connects Black Jack Campground to Middle Ranch Road.

CRESCENT AVENUE: The main street between Avalon Bay's beach and the city of Avalon's businesses was so named because of its arc shape, following the bay's contour. It is invariably known by residents and tourists alike by its nickname: Front Street.

D

DEER VALLEY RESERVOIR: This is a small pond along Little Harbor Road. It's one of very few nomenclature recognitions of the island's mule deer herd. The deer were introduced to the island in the 1920s and '30s for hunting purposes, ostensibly to draw more tourists.

DEFOREST, DR. LEE: From 1904 to 1905, under the auspices of the Banning brothers, DeForest developed the Audion vacuum tube, patented in 1907 and essential to radio technology, revolutionizing twentieth-century communication.

DESCANSO BEACH: The next harbor north of Avalon, around Casino Point, is a favorite spot for residents and visitors alike to "put a drink in their hand and their feet in the sand." The Descanso Beach Club bar and restaurant is operated by the Santa Catalina Island Company.

DESCANSO CANYON: Hancock Banning built his island home in this area in 1895. When the Hotel St. Catherine was built on the site in 1918, he moved his home farther up the canyon. This second residence later became a dormitory for the hotel staff. There was a tunnel through the hillside that connected Descanso to Sugarloaf Point, where the Casino is situated. A zip line experience built by the Santa Catalina Island Company in 2010 concludes at the canyon floor.

DIVIDE ROAD: The road along the ridgeline west and parallel to Avalon Canyon.

E

EAGLE ROCK: This small rock above the tide line is located just east of the island's East End on the south side. It is a popular site for divers.

EAGLE'S NEST LODGE: This structure in Middle Ranch Canyon was built between 1896 and 1898 by the Banning brothers as a hunting lodge and stagecoach stop. Its name comes from two bald eagles that nested in a tree near the lodge. Construction materials were shipped from the mainland and carried by mule to the building site. The lodge was originally a wooden two-room affair with a stone fireplace. A kitchen and shed were later added. By 1898, Stagecoach Road, aka Stage Road, was complete from Avalon to Two Harbors, and the site served as a way station for cross-island trips. During stops, horses were changed and guests enjoyed lunch. Just after Labor Day 1927, the lodge officially opened as the hunting

The stagecoach afforded tourists a prime view of Avalon Harbor. A stop on the way to Two Harbors was at Eagle's Nest Lodge in the interior. *Courtesy of Marvin Carlberg.*

headquarters. After World War II, the Santa Catalina Island Company instituted the Inland Motor Tour with the lodge as a stop for coffee and doughnuts. On May 15, 1984, the last official tour stop was made at the lodge. Storms in 1995 washed out the road to the lodge. Large repair equipment could not reach the site, and the lodge deteriorated. The refurbished road was finished in 2001.

EAGLE'S NEST PEAK: This peak near Middle Ranch has an elevation of 1,076 feet.

EAST END: The island region that contains Avalon and its environs extends as far west on the north shore as Gallagher Beach and back along the southern coast to the Palisades. East End Road is a dirt road between Renton Mine Road and Divide Road, creating with Stagecoach Road a vehicular loop on the hills above and around Avalon.

EAST MOUNTAIN: The twin bump with East Peak rises 1,563 feet above sea level from Jewfish Point and Seal Rocks at the island's easternmost points.

EAST PEAK: The highest point on the island's East End rises to 1,684 feet above sea level about a mile and a half south of Avalon. Not to be confused with adjacent East Mountain.

EAST SUMMIT: Very near Wrigley Reservoir, this rise at 1,450 feet above sea level is the place where Stagecoach Road ceases a two-mile switchback climb from Hogsback Gate up out of Avalon and begins to level off across the high terrain of the island.

EASTWOOD, ALICE: This Canadian-born botanist was the procurator and head of the Department of Botany at the California Academy of Sciences in San Francisco for more than a half century (1894–1949) and was a close friend of Catalina's intrepid botanist and poet Blanche Trask. Eastwood read the eulogy at Trask's funeral. She collected flowers on Catalina in 1917. F.A. Seavey, the first bug collector on Catalina, published his findings, "Insects of Catalina Island," in Eastwood's magazine, *Zoe*, in 1892.

ECHO LAKE: The only natural body of fresh water on Catalina Island, this small, isolated lake is located midway between White's Cove and the Airport in the Sky.

EMERALD BAY: Formerly known as Johnsons' Landing, Emerald Bay was renamed for the beautiful color of its crystal-clear waters, caused by the relatively shallow sandy bottom. It is a boating, snorkeling and diving destination with Indian Rock as the central point of interest. It has been home for the Boy Scouts of America since 1925 (with a hiatus during World War II). Today, the camp is operated by the scouts' Western Los Angeles Council.

EMPIRE LANDING: This bay on the north coast, about two miles from Isthmus Cove, is believed to once have been a large Tongva Native American town site, based on archaeological evidence. A large soapstone quarry was once located here, and it's thought that a Native American temple existed on the hill above.

F

FALLS CANYON: This is a watershed to the side of Avalon Canyon Road.

FELLOWS, DR. O.T.: A stone inn and way station overlooking Little and Shark Harbors on the overland stagecoach route from Avalon to Two Harbors was built by O.T. Fellows in the late 1800s.

FENCELINE ROAD: This steep mile-and-a-half dirt hiking trail links Silver Peak Trail with Parsons Landing and is a portion of the Trans-Catalina Trail.

FILMS AND TELEVISION: "Everyone making movies in Hollywood in the 1920s and 1930s spent some time at Catalina," wrote Lee Rosenthal in *Catalina in the Movies*. "And it's a good bet that more than a few scenes were shot on Catalina just to provide an excuse to be there." *Feeding the Seals at*

Catalina Isle (1910) was the first commercial film made on the island, and D.W. Griffith's *Man's Genesis* (1912) was the first fictionalized film. Calling attention to the island was the Fatty Arbuckle short *A Day at Catalina* (1914). Early versions of *Treasure Island* (1918), *Down to the Sea in Ships* (1922) and *The 10 Commandments* (1923) were made on Catalina. John Ford directed the 1931 movies *Men without Women* and *Seas Beneath* on Catalina. Errol Flynn starred in *Captain Blood* (1935) and *The Sea Hawk* (1940) with Catalina in the background. The local flavor also aided Edward G. Robinson in *Tiger Shark* (1932); Spencer Tracy in *Captains Courageous* (1937); Lana Turner in *Green Dolphin Street* (1947); John Wayne in *Wake of the Red Witch* (1948); Esther Williams in *Neptune's Daughter* (1949); Marlon Brando in *Morituri* (1965); Elvis Presley in *Easy Come, Easy Go*; and Rock Hudson and Jim Brown in *Ice Station Zebra* (1968).

Modern-day big productions that used the island include Steven Spielberg's *Jaws* (1975) and *Amistad* (1997), Kevin Reynolds's giant flop *Waterworld* (1995) and Michael Bay's *Pearl Harbor* (2000). *Mutiny on the Bounty* (1935) was the one Academy Award–winning best picture shot on Catalina. Stanley Kramer's *Bless the Beasts and the Children* (1971) used the island's bison herd. Director Roman Polanski shot some of *Rosemary's Baby* (1968) on the island and went back for *Chinatown* (1974). More than 250 movies have been lensed on the island. As for TV shows, they include *Cannon, Quincy M.E., The A-Team, Airwolf* and many others.

FIRE OF 1915: The granddaddy of fires on Catalina was the blaze on November 29, 1915, that destroyed about one-third of Avalon. In the early morning hours of November 29, residents were roused from their sleep by cries of "Fire! Fire!" and saw the city in flames. Many evacuated to what is now the Cabrillo Mole on the west side of the city and up Stagecoach Road into the hills. A faulty kitchen at a café in or near the Rose Hotel (today, the site of Hotel Villa Portofino) was blamed. However, an eyewitness to the blaze, Johnny Windle, a founding citizen, told how fellow residents Tinch Moricich and Squirrel D'Arcy rescued a woman from the attic of the Rose Hotel. Moricich, who later became town constable, said the attic door was intentionally locked. Moricich said he had to break a padlock and force open a trapdoor, injuring his shoulder. Windle said the woman's son-in-law had been moving his belongings out of the hotel in the days before the fire.

Only four hours before the fire, another mysterious fire was started on the other end of town, at 200 Eucalyptus Street, sending all of Avalon's volunteer firefighters across town. "Let me get this straight then," community historian Chuck Liddell said to Windell, "we're assuming [the son-in-law] locked the mother-in-law in there to do away with her." "You can assume what you want," Windell replied. The Los Angeles County district attorney investigated the story but without results. More than $2 million in property was lost. The Banning brothers tried to rebuild the town and added the Hotel St. Catherine at Descanso Beach. But a lack of funds and tourism during World War I forced them to sell the island in 1919 to a consortium of investors, which included chewing gum magnate William Wrigley Jr., who then eventually bought out his partners.

FIRE OF 2007: Of 299 fires recorded on the island during the last one hundred years, only six started from natural causes. The 2007 fire that threatened Avalon charred 4,700 acres, with several structures lost. It took a week to contain with off-island resources. It started on May 10 in the hills north and west of Avalon, at the broadcast towers of radio station KBRT. The destruction was primarily in Falls Canyon and Bird Park Canyon, south of downtown Avalon. Nearly three hundred firefighters battled the flames, arriving by hovercraft and Marine Corps helicopters. The Catalina Express operated all night, bringing seven hundred evacuees to Long Beach. Investigators charged Gary Dennis Hunt, a subcontractor working on the radio antennae guy wires with a torch, with accidentally starting the fire. On February 4, 2009, Hunt pleaded no contest to the charges and was sentenced to five years' probation, plus 720 hours of community service, ninety days in jail or Caltrans service.

FISHMAN, LEO: Leo "Duke" Fishman (1906–1977) was born in the Philippines to American parents. Orphaned at an early age, Fishman was raised in Australia by a relative. It wasn't long before the energetic young man was island hopping across the Pacific Ocean, landing in Avalon in 1935. His toned, bronzed physique; shaved head; jaunty captain's hat; and gold earring made a lasting impression on all who knew him. He taught the local kids how to swim and was credited by the *Catalina Islander* with having saved more than one thousand lives in his role of lifeguard. However, his greatest role was that of "Official Greeter." His heartfelt, "Hi, naybor!" charmed visitors as they disembarked from the steamer pier. The city council officially dubbed him "Mr. Catalina," although everyone knew him as the "Duke of Catalina."

From the 1930s through the 1950s, Fishman was a favorite of Hollywood filmmakers who filmed on the island, and he performed stunts or acted in *Mutiny on the Bounty* (1935), *The Ten Commandments* (1956), *Some Like It Hot* (1959), *Spartacus* (1960), *Irma La Douce* (1963) and *Planet of the Apes* (1968). He had guest roles on television's *Gunsmoke*, *I Spy*, *Lost in Space* and *Quincy*

M.E. An urban legend claims that Duke was the prototype for Proctor & Gambles' "Mr. Clean." When six-foot-four Catalina frequenter John Wayne was on the island, the pals were "Big Duke" and "Little Duke." Fishman stood five feet, six inches. During the mid-century, Avalon virtually closed down in the fall and winter, which Fishman spent in Palm Springs, where he died of a heart attack at the age of seventy-one. In April 1978, his ashes were returned to Catalina Island and interred in the Avalon Cemetery. Elizabeth Grierson wrote a biographical monograph— "Hi, Naybor!"—in his memory.

FLOATING PALACE: This was probably the first liquor barge on the West Coast. It replaced Billy's Place, operated by Billy "Bruin" Brohan, when authorities closed it during the development of the island by George Shatto. Billy's Place was euphemistically known as a hardware store, ostensibly owned by George Bryant, but was more of a hard liquor bar. The Floating Palace, owned by Bryant and Henry Crocker, was adorned with a large sign, "Hardware," but it was mostly a booze barge. When the Banning brothers bought the island, bartender Brohan and his sidekick, John "Chicken Johnnie" Brinkley (see Hermit Gulch), moved their operations inland. Brohan died in 1910 in Los Angeles.

FOURTH OF JULY COVE: One year, the Banning family decided to picnic in the pleasant little cove just west of the Isthmus. The holiday at that cove became a family tradition. Because of those outings, the Bannings named the inlet Fourth of July Cove. Today it is home to the Fourth of July Yacht Club.

FOX LANDING: The first cove east of Long Point on the leeward side of the island is presently a youth camp operated by Catalina Island Marine Institute (CIMI).

FROG ROCK: A small beach east of Descanso Beach features this prominent rock, which some say resembles its namesake amphibian. It's a popular kayak destination.

G

GALLAGHER BEACH: This small beach two miles northwest of Avalon was named after San Clemente Island sheepherder Tom Gallagher, who moved his business to Catalina in the 1860s.

GAMBEL, WILLIAM: Gambel (June 1823–December 13, 1849) was an American ornithologist and medical doctor who was the first to collect flora samples on Catalina Island from 1841 to early 1842. His friend Thomas Nuttal, considered the best field naturalist of the time, presented Gambel's work to the Philadelphia Academy in 1847. Nuttall honored Gambel by designating a new genus, *Gambelia*, for one of Gambel's plants from Catalina Island. Other namesakes include the oak *Quercus gambelii* and quail *Callipepla gambelii*. Gambel then went on to receive a medical degree from the University of Pennsylvania in 1848. He was twenty-five years old. Wanderlust and the discovery of gold at Sutter's Mill eventually got the best of him, and he began his journey west again. In poor health, he eventually made it to present-day Quincy in Plumas County, California. Typhoid fever was rampant in the mining camps. He began treating the miners and eventually contracted the disease himself. He died at the age of twenty-six in Rose's Bar.

GANO, PETER: Gano (b. circa 1840) built Avalon's oldest remaining structure, the Holly Hill House, the one with the round turret-shaped aspect on the hill above Pebbly Beach Road on the walk into Avalon from the Cabrillo Mole. He purchased the lot for $500 from George Shatto and his agent, C.A. Sumner, in 1888. As a civil engineer, Gano had the knowledge to build his dream home, which he dubbed Look Out Cottage. He brought the material over on his boat and then hauled it up the steep hill with the help of an old circus horse named Mercury. The horse powered a pulley system that moved the materials to the top. Once the home was completed in 1889, he is said to have invited his one true love to come and live with him. Gano had met her in Pasadena while working with the city on water rights. Apparently, the island did not hold the same romantic charm for her as it did for him, as she declined his invitation. It is said that Gano remained a bachelor until his death. Perhaps a bit soured by the experience, he reportedly posted signs around the property that read, "No Women Allowed."

GARBAGE: On an island, there's the constant reminder of what to do with waste, since limited space exists in which to place it. Several ancient trash dumps, or middens, exist on the island that date back to the early Native American people, the Tongva, who lived here. In the early 1900s, without today's sensibilities, those sites were picked over by collectors, who then displayed and sold these treasures of soapstone bowls, bones and religious relics. Similarly, old hunting campsites, especially where outhouses once stood, became interesting places to find bits of history as well. Archaeology students from the University of California Los Angeles and UC Northridge come to the island yearly to work and study. Today, a

Avalon's oldest remaining structure, the distinctive Holly Hill House with its red aspect roof, in the right corner of this image, was built on a lot purchased for $500 from George Shatto and his agent, C.A. Sumner, in 1888. Peter Gano, an engineer, built the house by himself, hauling material he had brought on his boat up the hill with the help of an old circus horse named Mercury. When the home was completed in 1889, he asked the woman he loved to join him. She refused to move to an island, and he remained there alone. Recently restored, the Holly Hill House is a conspicuous Avalon landmark. *Courtesy of Marvin Carlberg*

Holly Hill House is deep into its second century overlooking the city of Avalon. The original builder and homeowner Peter Gano is said to have posted "No Women Allowed" signs around the property after his love rejected his marriage proposal. *Photo by Justin Peter.*

managed landfill operates at Pebbly Beach on 7.7 acres, with 5.6 of that as landfill area. When work on the Wrigley Reservoir started in 2006, contractors were required to cut the old cover pieces into four-by-fives to match the size of the compressed bricks of garbage that go into the landfill. Recycling requires an extra step on the island, since it is barged back to mainland facilities.

GEOLOGY: Catalina is an oceanic island. The collision of two plates millions of years ago resulted in the formation of Catalina. The North American plate was moving from the mainland toward the sea while the Pacific plate was headed in the opposite direction. The two plates collided, causing the Farralon plate to slip under the North American plate. As the two upper plates slid, stretching and pulling the Earth's crust (just as it does at the San Andreas Fault today), a rupture occurred, and the schist from the lower Farralon plate pushed up with volcanic rock and ash to become Catalina Island. This means that Catalina's landmass was never directly connected to mainland California. Geologic uplift, tectonic plate movement, sedimentation, metamorphic activity, weathering and erosion all contributed to the formation of Catalina. Catalina is primarily composed of two distinct rocks—Catalina schist and igneous rocks—which jut out of the ground as outcroppings across the island. Catalina schist is from the early Cretaceous period, or between 109 to 95 million years ago. And the Miocene volcanic and intrusive igneous rocks date to the Miocene era, 23 to 5 million years ago. Quartz is plentiful, being the second most abundant mineral in the Earth's continental crust. Some beaches on the seaward side have silvery gray sand due to the abundance of quartz.

GHOSTS: Along with the tourists who hate to leave Avalon are a few locals and visitors who perhaps never left, at least in spirit. The Casino is a favorite ghost-spotting place for ethereal folks who, witnesses say, represent a variety of bygone eras in garb and usually vanish into thin air. Ghost Tours of Catalina is an established Avalon business, and such writers as *Catalina Islander* columnist Jim Watson and ghost book author Robert Wlodarski have expounded on individual ghost stories. The apparition of former Avalon resident Zane Grey, the western novelist and sports fisherman, has come in for his share of modern sightings.

GIBRALTAR BEACH: This is a boat-in campground on the leeward side of the island. The large rock at the beach was named for the gateway island to the Mediterranean Sea between Spain and Morocco.

GLASS-BOTTOMED BOATS: One of the early public attractions of Avalon were the glass-bottomed boat rides around Avalon Bay and Lovers Cove to view

Above: A glass-bottomed boat is depicted in 1904. In 1890, Charley Feige invented the first glass-bottomed boat to aid his abalone harvesting in the harbor by fitting a pane of glass into one of his rowboats. Feige gave up the abalone business and began taking eager tourists to see the undersea gardens. By 1900, glass-bottomed boat tours were among Avalon's most popular attractions. *Courtesy of Marvin Carlberg*

Left: A glass-bottomed boat investigates the submarine gardens of Lovers Cove. An artist's imagination provided the scene of the briny deep for this early twentieth-century postcard. *Courtesy of Marvin Carlberg*

fish and other undersea life. In 1890, abalone harvester Charley Feige used a box with a glass pane in the bottom that he held over the side of his boat to better see beneath the surface of Avalon Bay. He then installed a glass pane in the bottom of one of his rowboats. Tourism soon became a larger business for him than abalone. Captain J.E. "Pard" Mathewson arrived in Avalon in 1892, noticed Feige's enterprise and created bigger boats with bigger panes of heavy-duty glass in the bottom. In 1902, Mathewson debuted a thirty-eight-foot, gas-powered side-wheeler, the *Mon Ami*, a glass-bottomed boat that could carry fifteen passengers. Glass-bottomed boat tours became de rigueur for Catalina tourists in the twentieth century. Hollywood got into the act when Doris Day and Rod Taylor starred in the Avalon-set *The Glass Bottom Boat* (1966).

GLIDDEN, RALPH ARTHUR: Glidden (September 11, 1881–July 20, 1968) made his living unearthing Native American artifacts and human remains on Catalina Island and then offering them for sale and trade. In the 1930s, for thirty-five cents, the public could view his collection of oddities and curiosities in a museum situated on the western hillside of Avalon. The majority of Glidden's human collections are currently curated by the University of California Los Angeles. His artifacts included carved deer bones. Since the animals were brought to the island only in the 1920s and '30s, the carvings suggest they came from the mainland in trade for soapstone bowls and other commodities of the Tongva, who lived on Catalina into the 1820s.

GOAT HARBOR: This boat-in campground is located on the leeward side of the island. Feral goats were formerly a favorite hunting quarry on the island prior to their removal by the Catalina Island Conservancy and the Institute for Wildlife Studies.

GOAT WHISKERS TRAIL: This two-mile dirt trail on the West End connects the West End and Water Tower Roads with the Trans-Catalina Trail (Silver Peak Trail section) and Big Geiger Cove and Howland's Landing.

GOLF: The Catalina Golf Course was built in Avalon Canyon by the enterprising Banning brothers as a three-hole affair in 1892. Frank Whittley had built the Catalina Country Club structure in 1888. The golf course was the first west of the Mississippi River and one of the first in the United States. By 1894, the course had expanded to nine holes. The Bobby Jones Tournament was held there for years with the namesake golfing great participating. The course is known today as the Catalina Island Country Club.

GREEN PLEASURE PIER: The inner-bay pier in Avalon has been standing on the same spot for more than a century, facilitating tourism businesses and restaurants. It was constructed in 1909. (See piers.)

The Catalina Golf Course was built in 1892, making it the oldest golf course west of the Mississippi River. Originally designed as a three-hole course, it was expanded to nine holes in the early 1900s and eighteen holes later. During World War II, the course was neglected and brought back to nine holes in 1945. *Courtesy of Marvin Carlberg.*

In 1924, famous western novelist Zane Grey directed the construction of a large four-level structure in the style of the Zuni and the Hopi tribes of Pueblo Indians of the Southwest on a hilltop overlooking Avalon. Today, the Zane Grey Adobe is operated as a hotel with no connection to the Grey family. *Courtesy of Marvin Carlberg.*

GREY, ZANE: Grey (January 31, 1872–October 23, 1939) began life in Zanesville, Ohio, with the name of Pearl Zane Gray. He dropped the "Pearl" and changed the "a" to an "e" in his last name. Zane Grey attended the University of Pennsylvania on a baseball scholarship and became a dentist in New York City. He became a well-known author, writing action-packed western novels at the encouragement of his wife. In 1910, with the editorial help of his wife, Lina "Dolly" Roth, Grey wrote the bestselling novel *Heritage of the Desert*. He became one of the first millionaire authors, writing dozens of books. Many movie adaptations of his stories made it to the silver screen. After producing his best-known book, *Riders of the Purple Sage*, in 1912, he formed a motion picture company that he later sold to pioneering producer Jesse L. Lasky, a founding partner of Paramount Pictures. The bison herd currently on Catalina Island descended from animals brought to Catalina by the Lasky Film Company of Hollywood to make a film. Grey's novels include *The Vanishing American* (1925) and *Wild Horse Mesa* (1928). Grey was also an avid fisherman who reportedly fished some three hundred days out of the year and wrote several books on the subject. He was a member and one-time president of the Tuna Club in Avalon. His fishing books include *Tales of Fishes* (1919) and *Tales of Fresh Water Fishing* (1928). His home on Catalina Island is now the Zane Grey Pueblo Hotel, overlooking Avalon Harbor near the Chimes Tower.

H

HAMILTON COVE: Prior to becoming a private, gated residential development of condos and vacation rentals, this inlet north of Avalon and Descanso Beach once contained the old Amphibian Airport, where seaplanes landed and delivered mail and newspapers. The Amphibian Airport contained a circular turntable for repositioning seaplanes back toward the ocean. The cove was also once used as a boatyard. Ema I. Ritter's book, *Life at the Old Amphibian Airport*, contains much about this particular cove.

HAYPRESS RESERVOIR: Located at mile nine of the Trans-Catalina Trail, Haypress Reservoir was used as a "collecting center" for winter rainfalls. Haypress Picnic Area is a public playground and picnic site at the reservoir, maintained by the Avalon Lions Club.

Hamilton Cove, now the home of condominiums, was the site in the 1930s of the Catalina Airport for seaplanes. Its hangar was relocated to the Airport in the Sky in the late 1960s. *Photo by Justin Peter.*

HEN ROCK: A large boulder just off the shore between White's Landing and Fox Landing on the leeward side of the island resembles a fowl of the female persuasion.

HERMIT GULCH CAMPGROUND: John Brinkley (1887–1936), known to locals as "Chicken Johnnie," raised the birds that lent him his nickname around his isolated cabin at the junction of Avalon and Quail Canyons, today known as Hermit Gulch in his memory. Born in Suffolk, England, he arrived on Catalina in his mid-forties to build roads for George Shatto. His first home was near Avalon but was later relocated farther up the canyon when the Wrigley organization took over the island. When friends offered to build him new quarters and refurnish them, he declined. A scruffy figure in his later years, he bartered eggs, figs and fruit in Avalon for other staples using a wheelbarrow.

HOGSBACK GATE: This is the gate on Stagecoach Road out of Avalon into the interior. Only vehicles with permits from the Catalina Island Conservancy are able to enter Catalina's wild lands.

HOLDER, CHARLES FREDERICK: Holder (1851–1915) pioneered big game fishing in 1898, when he took a 183-pound blue fin tuna just off the

This busy beach scene in Avalon was captured in 1904. Mexican Joe's boathouse can be seen at the right. "Mexican Joe" Presciado was the boatman at the helm when Charles Frederick Holder—the founder of modern-day sport fishing—landed a six-foot, four-inch tuna weighing 183 pounds using a rod and six hundred feet of No. 21 line with a breaking strength of only 42 pounds. *Courtesy of Marvin Carlberg.*

shores of Catalina Island. He was the founder of the world's first sport fishing association, the Tuna Club of Avalon. He was the first major conservationist and sportsman to have a significant influence on Catalina. He established, in collaboration with the Banning brothers, the first zoological station on Catalina—the Banning Aquarium on the Avalon waterfront—in 1899. The Lynn, Massachusetts–born Quaker was assistant curator of zoology at the American Museum of Natural History in New York at age twenty. In Pasadena, Holder co-founded the Tournament of Roses and the Valley Hunt Club and taught zoology at Throop Polytechnic Institute, the forerunner of Cal Tech. He wrote at least seventeen books and hundreds of articles as a correspondent for *Scientific American*, the *San Francisco Daily Chronicle*, the *New York Times*, the *Boston Herald* and other publications. Many of these articles extolled the marine life off Catalina. His books include *An Isle of Summer, Santa Catalina; Its History, Climate, Sports, and Antiquities* (1901) and *The Channel Islands of California: A Book for the Angler, Sportsman and Tourist* (1910).

HOLLY HILL HOUSE: See Gano, Peter.

HOLLYWOOD'S BACKYARD: Catalina Island was a well-known hideout for Hollywood's elite, a playground for some and a respite for others. Many of the Hollywood set were weekend yachters, such as Humphrey Bogart and John Wayne, or sailors of some renown, such as Sterling Hayden and Johnny Weissmuller. After he starred in the film version of Zane Grey's *Riders of the Purple Sage* (1925), cowboy star Tom Mix bought a house on Maiden Lane in Avalon, not far from Grey's villa, and had installed a neon "TM" sign over the front awning, despite the objections of neighbors. Charlie Chaplin romanced Paulette Goddard at Avalon. Laurence Olivier and Vivien Leigh honeymooned on Catalina. Marilyn Monroe (Norma Jeane Mortenson) lived in Avalon for a time while her merchant marine husband, James Daugherty, was stationed on the island. One of the cases in the infamous trial for which Errol Flynn was acquitted for having sex with minors supposedly occurred on his yacht in Avalon Bay. Flynn and pal David Niven boated around the island on weekends. Wayne and Ward Bond hunted the West End. Victor McLaglen was a summertime resident. Robert Mitchum acted in the first legitimate stage play on the island. Depicted in notable photos with big fish caught off Catalina are Bing Crosby, John Barrymore, Stan Laurel and Frank Morgan. Others who enjoyed the island include Jean Harlow, Kate Smith, James Cagney, Warner Baxter, Mickey Rooney, Henry Fonda, Howard Hughes, Orson Welles, John Ford, Delores del Rio, Judy Garland, Andy Devine and aviation pioneer and one-time RKO Radio Pictures owner Howard Hughes. In the twenty-first century, Harrison Ford has been known to fly his plane into the Airport in the Sky, and the Catalina Film Festival has drawn such attendees as Sharon Stone and Patricia Arquette.

HOSPITAL: The first official Avalon clinic was established in 1915 in the Hotel Metropole but was as short-lived as the hotel, which, like a lot of the city, burned to the ground that November. After the city recovered, one Dr. Chapman saw patients in the Strand Hotel. Then the old Banning residence on Sumner Avenue was converted into a hospital of sorts, which served the island into the late 1950s. A community-wide effort was launched to finally create and establish a hospital at the fork of Avalon Canyon and Falls Canyon Roads: six beds, emergency and operating rooms, X-ray facilities, a laboratory, an observation room, a kitchen and a lobby. Expansions of the Catalina Island Medical Center occurred in 1984, with physical therapy and more administrative room, and again in 2003.

HOTEL METROPOLE: This was Avalon's first big building and most notable landmark throughout the nineteenth century. It opened for business for

Promotion of Santa Catalina Island as a resort was a constant in island history. This brochure is from 1949. *Courtesy of Marvin Carlberg*

the summer of 1888, the first year that Catalina was really marketed by George Shatto and his business associate, Charles Sumner, as a resort. By far the biggest building in town at three stories and nearly a block wide, it faced Avalon Bay on Crescent Avenue between Whittley and Metropole Avenues. After the Banning brothers took over ownership of the island, the Metropole added two additional wings of rooms, as well as a tennis court. Visitors for three decades either stayed at the Metropole or pitched tents behind it or down the beach. The Metropole remained Avalon's most dominant landmark until it was destroyed in the great fire of 1915. It was rebuilt for succeeding generations and has remained one of Avalon's most notable businesses.

HOTELS: The fire of 1915 became a renewal phase for hotels, which crowded the city of Avalon. The fire, which started suspiciously at the Rose Hotel at about 4:00 a.m. on November 29, quickly spread to other wooden structures in town, destroying the Hotel Metropole, Hotel Grandview,

New hotels in Avalon are advertised. All outside rooms were one dollar a day and up. All rooms featured hot and cold running water. Some rooms had baths and steam heat. *Courtesy of Marvin Carlberg.*

Hotel Park, Bay View Hotel, Hotel Catalina, Hotel Central, Hotel Miramar, Hotel Sea View and the J.J. Nestell Flats. In 1917, the Banning brothers, hoping to restore the glamour lost to the fire, constructed the Hotel St. Catherine on Descanso Beach. When William Wrigley Jr. took control of the island, he commissioned the building of the Hotel Atwater, named for Helen Atwater, daughter of Bert L. Atwater, who was for many years New York manager of the William Wrigley Jr. Company. At the outbreak of World War II, the island was closed to tourists and was used by the military. Facilities adapted on the island included a U.S. Maritime Service training facility in Avalon. Hotels such as the St. Catherine, the Atwater and many others were used to house the army, navy and U.S. Coast Guard troops sent to the island to train. The St. Catherine did not open again as a hotel until 1957 and was then razed in 1966.

HOTEL ST. CATHERINE: This jewel of hospitality was deemed to be one of the world's most luxurious resort hotels after it was completed in 1918 on lands owned by Hancock Banning in the bay front of Descanso Canyon. It was the most lavish attempt by the Banning brothers to reinvigorate the island in the World War I years, after the devastating Avalon fire of 1915 and just before William Wrigley Jr. bought the island in 1919. Most movie stars who came to the island to make pictures stayed at the St.

This view from above the Hotel St. Catherine looks toward Sugarloaf Casino and Little Sugarloaf Rock. *Courtesy of Marvin Carlberg.*

Catherine. It boasted a swimming pool, tennis courts, private cottages on the grounds, a posh dining room and the extremely popular Cocktail Corral bar. Secluded around the corner of what became Casino Point on Descanso Bay, the hotel also had a beautiful beach. The St. Catherine was used to house troops during World War II and never really regained its luster after the war. It was torn down in 1966.

HOWLAND'S LANDING: William Howland, who grazed large herds of cattle and sheep on Catalina, was one of the island's earliest settlers. This inlet is located on the north side of the West End a few miles northwest of Two Harbors.

HUNTING: Wild game wasn't really a provision of Mother Nature on Catalina but a human endeavor. Eagle's Nest Lodge was established in 1894 in Middle Ranch Canyon as a respite for both goat hunting parties and stagecoach passengers traversing the island. By the 1920s and '30s, mule deer had been brought over from the mainland for hunting as another way to entice tourists to the island. The most notable hunting photo that has endured in Catalina lore depicts Errol Flynn and archer Howard Hill dragging a dead boar up out of an island ravine. Exotic species were brought to Catalina in the late twentieth century with hopes of establishing a game reserve, which never quite panned out. Blackbuck antelope, native to the Indian subcontinent, were brought to the island in 1967. At the writing of this book, only a few males remain on the island. More than two thousand mule deer roam the island today, and deer tags are issued annually to hunters on Catalina.

1

INDIAN ROCK: This large rock off Emerald Bay is a popular diving spot.

INSECTS: More than forty-five species and subspecies of endemic invertebrates exist on Catalina. Among them are the Catalina shieldback katydid (*Neduba propsti*), Jerusalem cricket (*Stenopelmatus*; the Catalina version is yet unnamed by science), Catalina walkingstick (*Pseudosermyle catalinae*), painted tiger moth (*Arachnis picta meadowsi*) and Catalina orange tip butterfly (*Anthocharis cethura catalina*). Among the spiders is the California trapdoor spider (*Bothriocyrtum californicum*).

INSTITUTE FOR WILDLIFE STUDIES (IWS): Incorporated in 1979 as a nonprofit, with an office on Catalina, IWS is dedicated to long-term studies of specific species in relation to their environments. IWS, with support from the Catalina Island Conservancy, restored the bald eagle to a healthy breeding population on Catalina. IWS also worked with the Catalina Island Conservancy to bring the federally endangered Catalina Island fox back from the brink of extinction—from an outbreak of canine distemper. Both are among the more remarkable wildlife restoration stories of the twenty-first century. IWS also took the lead in removing the feral goats and pigs from Catalina.

IRON BOUND BAY: Located on the windward side of the West End, this notable inlet is between Ribbon Beach and Ribbon Rock.

IRONWOOD: More than one hundred ironwood groves exist on Catalina Island. According to a paper published by Catalina naturalist and newspaper columnist Bill Bushing in 1997, the Catalina ironwood (*Lyonothamnus floribundus floribundus*) and the closely related Santa Cruz ironwood (*Lyonothamnus floribundus asplenifolius*) are currently narrowly restricted endemics, limited in distribution to Catalina Island and to neighboring Santa Cruz, Santa Rosa and San Clemente Islands, respectively. Researchers say these two species had widespread distributions throughout the western United States during the Miocene era, based on fossil material dated from nineteen to six million years ago. One big ironwood grove exists on Catalina in Swain's Canyon, between Airport Road and Toyon Bay. Researchers suggest that the ironwood was eliminated from the mainland United States due to climatic changes in the late Miocene and Pliocene periods, which resulted in a drier climate with less summer rainfall. For this reason, these two taxa are referred to as relict endemics or paleoendemics.

ISLAND EXPRESS HELICOPTERS: Island Express has been operating tours, charters and exclusive Catalina Island trips since 1982. The company services all of Southern California, with exclusive-use heliports at the Queen Mary in Long Beach and the Catalina Cruise terminal in San Pedro. In April 2013, a new terminal was opened at Orange County Airport. Island Express flies three six-passenger helicopters that are turbine powered. It also has its own maintenance facility at Long Beach Airport.

ISTHMUS COVE: This big inlet on the north coast of the West End is the entrance to Two Harbors and, with Catalina Harbor on the windward side of the island, the bay that gives that unincorporated town its very name. A favorite filming spot for Hollywood over the years, Isthmus Cove is also a favorite anchoring spot, both literally and figuratively, for those who believe Avalon has too much hustle and bustle in the busy season. There's some reason to believe that this cove—and not

Avalon Bay—was where William Shaler repaired the *Leila Byrd* in 1804, naming the place "Port Roussellon," a moniker that never stuck. J.B. Banning built a wharf at the Isthmus in 1903 and his hacienda there in 1909. He envisioned a town on the Isthmus to rival Avalon, which was going to be called "Catalina City." But the sleepy little hamlet of Two Harbors prevailed. Once known as Union Harbor, Isthmus Cove has a colorful pre-twentieth-century history of pirates, smugglers, land barons, possibly Sir Francis Drake, Abraham Lincoln and, later, bootleggers and Hollywood. One of Catalina's most authoritative historians, Charles Frederick Holder, believed that Drake spent the winter of 1579 in Catalina Harbor, overhauling the *Golden Hind* after plundering Spanish towns and ships on his way up the west coast of Mexico. There is no doubt at all, however, that Catalina Harbor and other coves on the seaward side of the island have been favorite haunts of opportunists engaging in illegal actions over the centuries.

Near the center of the Isthmus is the barracks that was built on orders from President Lincoln during the Civil War. At that time, the coves and valleys on either side of the Isthmus were the center of intense, but supposedly never too successful, prospecting for gold, silver and galena (lead ore).

Tent cabins are for rent at the isthmus campground. Camping, and especially youth camping, remains extremely popular on Catalina. *Photo by Justin Peter.*

Many of the 1,200 claimholders were Southerners who made no secret of their support for the Confederacy. Lincoln, who said that he could not finance the Union cause without gold shipments from California, was said to be afraid that the pro-Secessionist miners might try to seize one of the ships carrying ingots from San Francisco when its passage south brought it near the island or into one of its coves. A barracks was built in January 1864. An infantry company of 80 men and 3 officers took up station, and cannons were put in place on the high ground to defend the harbors. The troops, however, were withdrawn after less than a year. During World War II, the Isthmus became a training center for the U.S. Coast Guard. Many hundreds of recruits slept in the old barracks after spending their days learning seamanship aboard a flotilla of eight schooners and four small whaling ships.

ITALIAN GARDENS: Located on the northern coast around Long Point from Avalon, this favorite angling bay of Italian fishermen out of San Pedro was named by them for their great fishing success there. It is today a boat-in campsite.

J

JEWFISH POINT: A popular diving spot on the far East End, this point is located just north of the quarry. "Jewfish" had been a nickname for an Atlantic Ocean fish, the Goliath grouper, and was indiscriminately applied to other species, such as the giant black sea bass.

JOURNALISM: The *Jewfish* was the island's first newspaper, published in 1892, followed by the *Avalon Avalanche* in 1893 and the *Avalon Crusoe* in 1903—all short-lived ventures. The *Wireless* was an early Avalon newspaper that was often critical of the Bannings and pushed for incorporation of Avalon as a city. It was published by Avalon businessman Willis LeFavor from 1912 to 1916. The *Catalina Islander* began publishing in 1914 as a counterforce against criticisms of the Banning operations. Issues of the day pitted the townsfolk, who wanted a "wet" city (with alcohol consumption) and no harbor commerce control versus the Bannings, who maintained a "dry" town and trade control over boat traffic. The *Islander* endured even as the Bannings lost on both counts when Avalon incorporated as a city. A century old, with a twenty-first-century circulation of five thousand, the *Islander* is distributed each Friday. The competition is the three-thousand-circulation *Avalon Bay News*, founded in 1990.

K

KBRT Tower: Once located along the Airport Road, just south of Middle Ranch Road, this giant antenna endured to 2013 as a remnant of bygone communications days. The tower once served KBIG, one of the highest-rated musical stations in the country, founded by John H. Poole in 1952 on the AM dial. Known as the "Catalina Island Station," KBIG carried unique programming boosted by magnified signal strength, which Poole knew would be achieved by broadcasting the station's directional signal across ocean water from San Diego to Santa Barbara. Adhering to an island theme, KBIG scheduled music, news and commercials on a sequence different from competitors. "We knew if you changed stations during a commercial, you would always find music on KBIG," Poole claimed. The call letters were named in honor of the station's original disc jockey, Carl "Mr. Big" Bailey. Big band music and new hits were the station's métier. The operation was sold to religious broadcasters in 1980, which operated as KBRT. In 2013, KBRT relocated its transmitter to Anaheim. The KBRT antenna array was "ground zero" for the May 2007 fire that threatened Avalon. A subcontractor's tools ignited the blaze.

Kelp Point: Located on the leeward side of the West End, west of Cat Harbor, this is a favorite diving area accessible by boat only. Giant kelp forests grow just off Catalina and are home to sea lions, abalone, giant sea bass, lobster and other marine creatures.

L

Land's End: As if pointing northwest out into the seeming infinity of the Pacific blue, this wild, windswept strip of land is the westernmost point of the island.

Laura Stein Volunteer Camp: Located across Stage Road from the Haypress Reservoir, this camp serves as a home to visiting volunteer groups. The camp's namesake accepted a position in 1992 with the Catalina Island Conservancy as its first coordinator of Volunteer and Membership Services. She built the department with local and mainland volunteers and the conservancy's support groups to organize dozens of special events and activities. Stein was killed in an island vehicle accident on May 27, 1993. The volunteer camp, funded by conservancy board member Norris Bishton, was dedicated on June 12, 1994.

LAVA WALL: This boat-in campsite on the leeward side of the island between Paradise Cove and Gibraltar Beach has long been a favorite for kayak campers. It is backed by an impressive, vertical wall of rock that provides cool shade in the afternoons.

LICK, JAMES: Lick (August 25, 1796–October 1, 1876) was an American carpenter, piano builder, land baron and patron of the sciences. He was born in Lebanon County, Pennsylvania; spent some years in South America; and came to San Francisco before the gold rush. At the time of his death, he was the wealthiest man in California and left the majority of his estate to social and scientific causes. Ever since Governor Pío Pico made a Mexican land grant of Catalina to Tomas M. Robbins in 1846, the island was sold and resold, first to Jose María Covarrubias in 1850, then to Albert Packard of Santa Barbara in 1853 and, finally, in 1864 to Lick. However, when Lick died in 1876, the island reverted to the Lick estate.

In 1887, George Shatto purchased the island from the Lick estate for $200,000. Because of some shady financial arrangement with an English syndicate, Shatto quickly found himself way over his head in debt to the Lick Foundation. Since 1889, the Banning brothers had been working secretly with the estate to make good the payments that Shatto had been unable to meet. When Shatto realized that the end of his ownership had come, he accepted the $25,000 from the Bannings to buy up the Avalon lots that had yet to be sold. The Bannings then paid off the remaining debt of $126,727.28 to the Lick estate. This money helped build the California Academy of Sciences Building on Market Street in San Francisco. Among Lick's lasting achievements was financing the University of California's Lick Observatory, which was completed in 1888 in the Diablo Mountains east of San Jose.

LION HEAD: This prominent rock outcropping marks the westernmost boundary of Fourth of July Cove on the island's West End. It's a popular dive site with giant kelp forests.

LITERATURE: Catalina has inspired quite a few writers, foremost among them the former internationally celebrated residents Charles Frederick Holder, natural history maven; Gene Stratton-Porter, the Indiana-born author of the popular novels *Freckles* (1904) and *A Girl of the Limberlost* (1909); and Zane Grey, the western novelist whose dozens of novels include *Riders of the Purple Sage* (1925). Holder, who extolled the isle in several books and many dozens of articles, wrote what appears to be the first widely distributed novel about Catalina, a young-adult story, *The Adventures of Torqua*, which contained the explanatory subtitle: *Being the Life and Remarkable Adventures of Three Boys, Refugees on the Island of Santa Catalina (Pimug-na) in the Eighteenth Century*. It was published in Boston by Little, Brown in 1902. The twentieth-century Catalina-set literature includes Charlotte Herr's *Their Mariposa Legend: A Romance of Santa Catalina* (1921) and Louise O'Flaherty's *House of the Lost Woman* (1974). Recent literature includes *Mercy of the Elements* (2011) by Christopher Blehm and *Catalina Summer* by Gil Lefebvre.

LITTLE FISHERMAN'S COVE: The site of the USC Wrigley Institute for Environmental Studies is located immediately northwest of Isthmus Cove. In 1965, Philip Wrigley dedicated five and a half acres of this cove to the University of Southern California to create an island marine science center.

LITTLE HARBOR: A windward inlet that shares its bay with Shark Harbor, divided by a rock formation called the Whale's Tail, this picturesque spot was once an ancient Native American town site and the location of an inn, built by Dr. O.T. Fellows in 1894, serving the cross-island stagecoach line. Little Harbor Overlook is located on a promontory above Little and Shark Harbors, providing breathtaking views of the two neighboring harbors, as well as Catalina Harbor in the distance and a pristine stretch of the leeward side of the West End from Lobster Bay to Ribbon Rock. Isthmus Road is a five-mile stretch of dirt road leading north from Little Harbor to the Isthmus. It connects on the southern end with Middle Ranch Road and El Rancho Escondido Road.

LITTLE SPRINGS CANYON: This watershed just above Little Harbor is flanked on the west by the Trans-Catalina Trail and to the east by Little Harbor Road.

LIVESTOCK: The Spanish and other explorers were thought to have started releasing or raising livestock on Catalina in the two centuries between Vizcaino's discovery of the island in 1602 and Mexico's revolt from New Spain in 1820. A notable goat-hunting guide for decades in the later 1800s and early 1900s was Jose "Mexican Joe" Presciado. By the time of the American Civil War, Union army estimates put fifteen thousand sheep and eight thousand goats on the island. These animals decimated native flora in a time when that or other ecological issues weren't general concerns. Cattle and pigs also scattered into the wild lands throughout the centuries. After the Catalina Island Conservancy was founded in 1972 and took control of 88 percent of the island in 1975, the feral livestock problem became amplified. To restore and preserve the flora and fauna, the remaining thousands of goats and pigs had to be removed, to the consternation of some locals, some of whom had previously and quietly hunted wild mutton and pork for sport and sustenance. The last feral goat was removed in 2004. One last boar, the so-called ninja pig, was known to still trample Catalina's wilds through 2013.

LOBSTER BAY: The first bay on the West End to the west of Catalina Harbor is named for the tasty crustacean that lives off Catalina's shores.

LONE TREE: This point above the Palisades on the southern coast of the island is situated just east of Silver Canyon Landing. It's about a mile west of Divide Road along Lone Tree Trail.

LONG POINT: The most prominent land formation on the north shoreline between Avalon and Two Harbors points directly east between Long Point Beach on the north and Fox Landing on the south.

Lovers Cove is shown along with the back side of the Intermountain Railway. Occasionally called Angels Flight, the name of a similar funicular in downtown Los Angeles, the Intermountain Railway's popularity was affected by the Avalon fire of 1915. *Courtesy of Marvin Carlberg.*

LOVERS COVE: In Avalon, this is the next cove to the east from Avalon Bay, along Pebbly Beach Road. A popular cove for glass-bottomed boats and semi-submersibles, this cove was the anchorage for the Chinese junk *Ning Po* when it operated as a Chinese restaurant prior to its move to Cat Harbor.

LOWER BUFFALO RESERVOIR: This is a man-made reservoir along Little Harbor Road on the East End approaching the Isthmus.

LOWER COTTONWOOD TRAIL: This five-and-a-half-mile dirt trail in Cottonwood Canyon begins at El Rancho Escondido and ends at Middle Ranch Road near Cottonwood Beach.

M

MAMMALS: Five land mammals are native: the Catalina Island fox (*Urocyon littoralis catalinae*), the Catalina California ground squirrel (*Otospermophilus beecheyi*), the Catalina Island harvest mouse (*Reithrodontomys megalotis catalinae*), the Catalina Island deer mouse (*Peromyscus maniculatus catalinae*) and the ornate shrew (*Sorex ornatus*). The Catalina subspecies of island fox was driven to the brink of extinction by an outbreak of canine distemper virus in 1999, when about 100 were thought to still be alive, mostly on the West End. The work by the Institute for Wildlife Studies and the Catalina Island Conservancy rallied to bring the animal back. About 1,800 were estimated to live in the wild lands, based on 2013 data. Nine shrews were sighted between 1941 and 2002. Three were captured in 2003 by the conservancy. Ornate shrews are smaller than some insects, difficult to capture and may survive in wetter areas of the island. The island is also home to a number of nonnative animals, notably the American bison (Bison bison). In 1924, 14 bison were brought to the island for the filming of the movie *The Thundering Herd* (1925). The film company left the bison on the island instead of bringing them back to the mainland. Today, the size of the bison herd is maintained at a population of about 150 animals. Other mammals on the island include more than 2,000 mule deer, which were brought over in the 1920s and '30s in an effort to gain tourism through hunting, as well as feral cats and rats. On the beaches and rocks, pinnipeds, such as California sea lions and harbor seals, warm themselves in the California sun.

Feeding the sea lions attracted tourists to Avalon Harbor, 1913. California sea lions and harbor seals are ubiquitous on Catalina's shores. *Courtesy of Marvin Carlberg.*

MARILLA STREET: This Avalon street is named after city developer George Shatto's sister-in-law, Etta Marilla Tichner Whitney.

MARINE LIFE: The waters surrounding Catalina famously teem with life, including fish such as the brilliantly orange and easily seen Garibaldi (the official California state marine fish), as well as yellowtail, California sheepshead, giant black sea bass, bat rays, leopard sharks, shovelnose guitarfish, white sea bass and many others. Albacore, marlin and swordfish attract deep-sea fishermen based at Avalon. Great white sharks have been caught off Catalina. Common marine mammals around Catalina include the pinnipeds, California sea lions and harbor seals.

MARTIN, GLENN L.: Martin (January 17, 1886–December 5, 1955) was one of aviation's great pioneers. He founded his own aircraft company in 1912, which later merged with the Wright company to become Lockheed Martin. In 1932, he was awarded the Collier Trophy for his work on the Martin B-10 bomber. Before fame and fortune, he was a young man intent on flying. His mother, Minta DeLong Martin, was his sponsor and staunch supporter. On May 10, 1912, he flew a pontoon-equipped, box-kite flying machine from Newport Bay to Catalina: thirty-four miles in thirty-seven minutes. This became the longest over-water flight up to that time, with the first on-water landing. Before he took off, historian Charles Hillinger wrote, Martin's mother noticed that one of the struts needed fixing. "Wait a minute, Glenn," she called. "I'll take a stitch in that thing. And while I'm doing it, you get home and put on your good suit. If you crack up in that ship I want you looking your best." He followed his mother's suggestion and returned later in a new suit of clothes. While he was gone, his mother took several stitches with heavy silk thread in the wobbly strut, reinforcing it with hairpins.

METROPOLE AVENUE: This street was named for the hotel that dominated Avalon; its name is derived from Old French based on Greek and means the "parent state of a colony," which, for all intents and purposes, the Hotel Metropole was in Avalon's nineteenth-century years.

MIDDLE RANCH: The original location for Middle Ranch, operated by the Banning brothers, who purchased the island in 1891 from George Shatto, was on the present site of Thompson Reservoir. That site contained a

A carriage tour rolls through Middle Ranch on the way to Eagle's Nest Lodge. Stagecoach drivers changed horses for fresh ones at the lodge. *Courtesy of Marvin Carlberg.*

barn and bunkhouses to support the newly formed Santa Catalina Island Company ranching interests. In 1924, under the direction of William Wrigley Jr., the barn and other buildings were moved to make way for the new 100-million-gallon reservoir to serve the growing population of Avalon. The reservoir is named after a Chicago water commissioner who designed the dam. Middle Ranch is now home to the Catalina Conservancy's Conservation and Facilities Departments and its Ackerman Native Plant Nursery. Middle Ranch Road is a ten-mile stretch of dirt road connecting Airport Road, just to the west of KBRT Ranch, to Little Harbor. The road was built between 1897 and 1898 by Samuel S. Farnsworth as part of the Avalon-to-Isthmus Stagecoach Road project.

MINING: The discovery of gold at Sutter's Mill in 1849 brought people from all over the world to California. However, as the dig in Northern California started playing out, miners set their sights on Santa Catalina Island. Between 1863 and 1864, dozens of silver and gold prospectors staked claims on the island. The mines were mostly on the West End in the vicinity of Cherry Valley and the Isthmus, but some were in Silver Canyon on the East End. Ships from San Francisco off-loaded supplies at Johnson's Cove—today's Emerald Bay—where streets were mapped for a town to be named Queen City. Miners discovered silver in 1864, but when the Union army occupied the island that same year, all but a few miners with substantial claims were forced to leave.

David Malcolm Renton, influential in the development of Catalina Island under William Wrigley Jr., most notably for overseeing the construction of the Avalon Casino, was interested in the possibility of mining on Catalina Island because of his experience with water well drilling. In 1923, he established a mine on Black Jack Mountain. His first shipment was about twenty tons of raw ore containing silver, lead and zinc. From February to November 1926, Renton manufactured and shipped close to three thousand tons of concentrates worth more than $90,000. In 1927, when mining operations temporarily ceased due to an international drop in ore prices, Renton constructed a one-hundred-ton floatation mill at White's Landing called "Silver Isle 100 Ton Flotation Mill." A wooden aerial cable tramway moved the ore from Black Jack to the mill in large metal buckets. At the time, salt water had not been used in flotation mills. Chemists advised that salt water would not work to separate minerals. But Renton discovered that kelp and saltwater organisms furnished the potassium iodide needed to separate minerals in salt water. Separating the concentrated ore was further helped by the

The residence of William Wrigley Jr. and his wife, Ada, was on a hilltop, which was later named Mount Ada. Built between March and December 1921, the home was designed by D.M. Renton and draftsman Walter Harris in Georgian Colonial design. From an elevation of more than three hundred feet, it overlooks Avalon Canyon, including the area where the Chicago Cubs spring training camp was located from 1921 until 1952 (except for the World War II years). *Courtesy of Marvin Carlberg.*

accidental addition of kerosene and linseed oil. Renton's mines yielded a respectful return for about two years. But the silver, zinc and lead finally played out. The profits from the mines were used to improve the standard of living for Avalon's population.

MOONSTONE COVE: Next to White's Landing, this inlet contains moorings for sixty boats and anchorage for fifty. The Newport Harbor Yacht Club has on-shore facilities at Moonstone Cove.

MOUNT ADA: Also known as Mount Buena Vista, "Ada" came in vogue after William Wrigley Jr. built his home near the top, overlooking Avalon, and named it for his wife.

MOUNT BANNING: This 1,734-foot peak is located a mile southwest of the island's highest point, the 2,097-foot-high Mount Orizaba, and between Cottonwood and Sweetwater Canyons.

MOUNT ORIZABA: The highest point on the island, at 2,097 feet above sea level, rises at the center of the island between Cottonwood and Cape Canyons.

MOUNT TORQUEMADA: Rising 1,336 feet above sea level over Lobster Bay, this promontory is the highest point on the island's West End. Possible nomenclature origins were with Tomas de Torquemada, the orchestrator of the Spanish Inquisition, or more likely, Sebastian Vizcaino's biographer and New Spain chronicler Fray Juan de Torquemada (circa 1562–1624).

N

Narbonne, Nathaniel Andrew: A native of Salem, Massachusetts, Narbonne moved to the Sacramento-area gold country, then to the present-day Lomita in 1852 and worked with General Phineas Banning in Wilmington before partnering with Ben Weston. They grew wheat and raised sheep on Catalina Island in the nineteenth century.

Native Americans: In prehistoric times, a group migrated to the southwest from the Great Plains and what is now Wyoming and settled in the area that became Los Angeles and Orange Counties. A portion of this population constructed canoes as long as twenty-five to thirty feet with a beam of five feet and crossed the channel to the southern Channel Islands. On Catalina, they called their new home Pimu or Pemú'nga. They were the Tongva. In 1542, when Juan Rodriguez Cabrillo first landed on the island, the Tongva greeted him. The canoes could carry up to fifteen people. These seaworthy crafts made travel and trade among the Channel Islands and the mainland fairly routine. The Tongva had dozens of communities across Pemú'nga, favoring the more sheltered north-facing canyons. The largest populations were found in Avalon Canyon and the Isthmus and at Little Harbor. Access to fresh water was a primary concern to the natives, who sought out larger canyons with streams that ran year round. They had a virtually unlimited supply of fish and shellfish. Acorns, wild onions and prickly pear rounded out their diet.

Pemú'nga also favored the Tongva with large quantities of steatite, also known as soapstone. This soft rock was easily mined from outcroppings in the canyons. The soapstone had a high talc component that rendered the rock heat resistant. Food could be cooked, keeping in the nutrition, contributing to the health of the community. Heat-resistant, virtually shatterproof cooking utensils, in addition to carved effigies, were the main export to tribes on the other Channel Islands in addition to the mainland. Soapstone bowls, jugs and other utensils have been found as far away as Oregon and Washington, as testament to their popularity. The Tongva worshipped a god named Chingichnich, in which elaborate rituals were conducted in large temples near the island's villages. There is speculation that these groups of believers were influenced by Christian practices introduced by Sebastian Vizcaino on his visit to the island in 1602.

NATURE CENTER AT AIRPORT IN THE SKY: Built in 1986, this outdoor exhibit includes the Soapstone Trail, tracing early Native Americans' industriousness using the namesake stone to fashion cookware.

NATURE CENTER AT AVALON CANYON: Built by the Los Angeles County Department of Parks and Recreation as a Channel Islands interpretive center, its management was transferred to the Catalina Island Conservancy, and it opened on Earth Day, April 22, 2006. This museum and gallery offers unique glimpses into Catalina natural history.

NOLAVA CANYON: Opposite Avalon Canyon on the windward side of the island, "Nolava" is also "Avalon" spelled backward.

NUTTALL, LAWRENCE WILLIAM: Nuttall (September 17, 1857–October 16, 1933) was an amateur botanist. In 1923, along with Charles Frederic Millspaugh, he produced a scholarly study, published by the Department of Botany at Chicago's Field Museum of Natural History, entitled *The Flora of Santa Catalina Island.* In the book, the authors identified 467 distinctive plants as occurring on the island. And as extensive as that work was, Nuttall's real interest was in the fungi of West Virginia. That's what put his name in the annals of botany. So passionate was he in his work that his son wrote that his father "went out every evening to gather plants and spent all of his spare moments in identifying his finds, among which were a couple of [species] that he could not identify...they were a new discovery." In 1927, Nuttall donated more than one thousand species of fungi, most of which were first described at his home in Fayette County, West Virginia, to the West Virginia University Herbarium. As an interesting side note, Lawrence William Nuttall and Thomas Nuttall, friend of William Gambel, were not related other than in terms of their interest in the plants of Catalina.

O

OLD BEN: This California sea lion (1899–1920) is immortalized in a bronze statute situated on the walkway from the Cabrillo Mole into Avalon. The Travillo brothers' circus act supposedly stayed on the island and trained

Old Ben was a large and friendly sea lion that came to Avalon Harbor in 1898. The town mooch, he flip-flopped through the streets, looking for snacks and posing for snapshots. He appeared in a 1914 movie, *The Sea Nymphs*, before disappearing in the early 1920s. *Courtesy of Marvin Carlberg.*

Old Ben, the sea lion, charmed tourists and residents. Avalon never forgot its town pet, and in 1975, the city erected a life-sized concrete statue of Old Ben at the end of the Cabrillo Mole. That statue was replaced by an identical one made of bronze in 1986, and in 2009, it was moved from its spot on the end of the pier to a more downtown location. *Courtesy of Marvin Carlberg.*

the sea lion. The Travillo kids would entertain tourists by diving for quarters tossed into Avalon Bay in the 1920s.

OLD EAGLE'S NEST TRAIL: This dirt trail leads from Eagle's Nest Lodge to Eagle's Nest Peak, which is 1,076 feet above sea level.

P

PALISADES: This name is given to the high, steep escarpments along the southern shore of the island's East End.

PARADISE COVE: Paradise Cove, also known as Cave Beach, is just east of Rippers Cove on the island's leeward side. It contains a boat-in campsite.

PARSONS' LANDING: This remote West End locale beyond Arrow Point from the Isthmus was named after Nathaniel Parsons, twin brother of Theophus Parsons, who built a stone house near the beach. He raised cattle and sheep and grew vegetables until he reached about eighty years of age, when he went to live with his sister in Los Angeles. Today, this remote campsite, along the Trans-Catalina Island Trail, provides hiking and kayaking opportunities.

Parsons' Landing is a remote campsite on the island's West End. The next stop is Starlight Beach for those traversing the Trans-Catalina Trail from east to west. *Photo by Justin Peter.*

PATRICK RESERVOIR: This pond is located six hundred feet southwest of the Haypress Reservoir Recreation Area along the Trans-Catalina Trail.

PATTON, GENERAL GEORGE S.: Patton (November 11, 1885–December 21, 1945) famously commanded the U.S. Third Army in Europe during World War II and was portrayed by George C. Scott in the Academy Award–winning film *Patton* (1970). Patton was a frequent visitor to Catalina in the late nineteenth and early twentieth centuries. His grandfather "Don Benito" Wilson was close friends with Phineas Banning and collaborated on the building of San Pedro Harbor. Hancock Banning was married to Patton's aunt, forming a close alliance between the two families. After the Bannings acquired the island in 1892, Patton's father purchased land and a cottage. From the age of ten through his teens, Patton spent several weeks on Catalina each summer.

PEBBLY BEACH: The rocky waterfront a mile south of Avalon was the site of an amphibious plane ramp, built in 1959, and is today the site for the City of Avalon's utilities power plants and landfill. Pebbly Beach Road, south from Avalon, hugs the seacoast past its namesake beach and down beyond Jewfish Point.

A fishing boat anchors off Pebbly Beach. The infrastructure hub for Avalon is located at Pebbly Beach, including an electric plant and intermittently operated desalination plant. It is also where the daily barge docks with supplies from the mainland and the heliport is located. Between 1959 and 1972, airline businesses flew amphibious aircraft to a seaplane ramp constructed at the site. *Photo by Justin Peter.*

PERDITION CAVE: Perdition Cave at Blue Cavern Point on the eastern edge of Isthmus Cove is large enough to accommodate a number of inflatable craft, as well as sea kayaks. In the musical *Jupiter's Darling* (1955), Hannibal's soldiers dive off Blue Cavern Point to capture Esther Williams. But the lithe swimming star easily loses her pursuers in the cave.

PIERS: Several piers were constructed in Avalon Harbor since the late 1800s. In 1887, George Shatto, a businessman from Michigan, purchased the island from James Lick of San Francisco. Shatto was the first owner who foresaw Catalina's worth as a resort venue. He built the Hotel Metropole and steamship pier, which would become Avalon's gateway for years to come. When the Banning brothers took over the island in 1892, they were determined to keep a "closed harbor," in which all tourist traffic could be regulated and controlled. A "parallel pier" was built in 1907, extending a few hundred feet from the beach and connecting the "Steamer Pier" to a small pier on the beachfront's south side. This infuriated the business community, as any attempt to impede the flow of tourists would also restrict their incomes. The Freeholders Improvement Association, composed of residents of Avalon, took the Bannings to court in protest. The Freeholders won their case, and the pier was dismantled. The planks were used to build the Pleasure Pier in 1909. The term "Pleasure" was immediately used to distinguish it from the Steamer Pier, controlled by the Bannings. The Pleasure Pier, which exists today, wasn't called the "Green Pleasure Pier" for a number of years, as it was originally painted beige.

PIMU: This was the name—occasionally cited as Pemú'nga—given to the island by the Native American Tongva tribe, who lived on the island as many as eight thousand years ago.

PIN ROCK: A small, narrow rock just inside Catalina Harbor.

PLANTS: About four hundred species of native plants grow on the island. Six species, subspecies or varieties are endemic and can be found only on Catalina Island: Catalina manzanita (*Arctostaphylos catalinae*), Catalina mountain mahogany (*Cercocarpus traskiae*), Catalina liveforever (*Dudleya hassei*), St. Catherine's lace (*Eriogonum giganteum* var. *giganteum*), Santa Catalina bedstraw (*Galium catalinense* ssp. *catalinense*) and Santa Catalina ironwood (*Lyonothamnus floribundus* ssp. *floribundus*). *Toyon* var. *macrocarpa*, or Christmas berry, is also a Santa Catalina endemic. These plants may be seen at the island's Wrigley Memorial & Botanic Garden.

POLICING THE ISLAND: The Freeholders Improvement Association, composed of Avalon residents, was established around the turn of the century to act as self-deputized enforcers of behavior in Avalon, according to Chuck

The Pleasure Pier, known today as the Green Pleasure Pier, was basically a gift to the city, having been sold to Avalon for the princely sum of five dollars in 1909. It was originally built by the Freeholders Improvement Association, a group of local businessmen. It was conceived as an alternative landing spot in opposition to an attempted monopoly by the Banning brothers, who had built a pier parallel to the beach in 1905 (and tried to corner most of the tourist business). *Courtesy of Marvin Carlberg.*

The Green Pleasure Pier serves as the dock for several of the more popular water activities like parasailing and glass-bottomed boat tours. It was originally built in the early 1900s by the Freeholders Improvement Association and then sold to the city of Avalon. *Photo by Justin Peter.*

Liddell, Avalon's de facto historian. Avalon had a constable going back to 1894. The first jail was built in 1896 and was a wooden structure measuring twelve by fourteen feet and apparently not very strong. In one story, the constable had incarcerated a peace disturber overnight. In the morning, he went to get his prisoner and met the man walking toward Avalon. The prisoner announced that he was thirsty and hungry so he knocked out a couple jail boards and freed himself. The constable chastised him and demanded that he repair the jail before he saw the judge later that day.

An official police force was established in 1920. However, the policemen were all Avalon residents—a fairly tight group given to protecting friends, family and one another. The police force was disbanded in favor of the Los Angeles County Sheriff's Department in 1960, following three annual "Buccaneer Days" festivals (not to be confused with the present-day Buccaneer Days in October at Two Harbors). Beginning in 1958, Avalon's Buccaneer days spanned a long weekend, encouraging bawdy pirate costumes and raucous partying and culminating in the Buccaneer Ball in the Avalon Casino Ballroom. In 1960, the fun got out of hand, becoming "a near riotous event," according to the *Catalina Islander*, with drinking, drug use and alleged gang rapes on Crescent Avenue. The Sheriff's Department was called in as backup to quell the violence, signaling the end of the Avalon Police Department. The LA Sheriff's Department took over in 1961.

POTTERY AND TILE: As legend has it, in 1926, William Wrigley Jr. and his second in command, David Malcolm "D.M." Renton, were out for an automobile ride near the Avalon golf course. It must have just rained because the car's tires became mired in mud. Renton, a builder, recognized the mud as a form of adobe. He suggested to his boss that the clay might be used to make bricks. Wrigley told the resourceful Renton to see what he could do using the island's clay. Renton's solution was the Catalina Tile & Pottery Company, which opened in 1927 on Pebbly Beach. The new pottery became Catalina Clay Products, a division of Wrigley's Santa Catalina Island Company. The pottery used local clay from the island, made useful building products and provided year-round employment for islanders. In 1930, artisans were added to the staff to design decorative and functional pottery products, including souvenirs, vases, bookends and figurines.

Red clay found on the island was used for pottery until 1931. After 1931, white clay from the United States mainland was combined with the red clay until, finally, only white clay was used. Glazes were made with local minerals mined on the island. The company sold its ware as Catalina Pottery and Catalina Tile, opening stores in Avalon and Hollywood. Dinnerware and art ware were sold through department and jewelry stores. The pottery's tile was used for the interiors and exteriors of buildings on the island. Tile products were used throughout the United States. The Arizona Biltmore Hotel's swimming pool in Phoenix was built using Catalina tile. In 1937, Catalina Clay Products, including all equipment, stock, molds and trademarks, was sold to the Gladding, McBean company, and the Catalina plant was closed.

PRENTISS, SAMUEL: Prentiss (1782–1854) was a Catalina legend. Much of the following information is unconfirmed, yet it makes for a great campfire tale. Prentiss, who is occasionally referenced as "Prentice," was a ship's carpenter on the brigantine *Danube*, out of New York. It wrecked on the rocks near San Pedro in 1824, often stated by history as December 1828. Prentiss, along with other sailors and survivors, walked to the San Gabriel Mission, where he became fast friends with an old Gabrielino Indian called Turei, supposedly a chieftain from Catalina. Turei, just prior to his death, told his younger friend great stories of Spanish treasure buried beneath a tree on the island. He sketched a map to the treasure that he gave to Prentiss, who returned to the *Danube* and salvaged enough material to build a small craft. Fate, though, was not on his side. Caught in a severe three-day storm in the middle of the San Pedro Channel on his way to the island, Prentiss lost everything, including the map. He eventually landed at what's now known as Emerald Bay. The legend says that he spent the next thirty years in a relentless and unsuccessful pursuit of the treasure but told no one of this until near death at the age of seventy-two. Even still, in an article printed in the *Catalina Islander* in July 1931, he was reportedly such a "friendly and goodnatured" fellow that a mining acquaintance carved an inscription on a board and placed it on his grave at Johnson's Landing (now Emerald Bay). It was later replaced with a tablet of stone, a donation by Judge Banning. Brickwork and a plaque dedicated to Catalina's "first white man" were added in 2003. The plaque states, "In memory of Samuel Prentice, a native of Massachusetts, arrived in California 1824, died on Catalina 1854, age 72 years." The legend, however, lives on. (See also Bouchette, Santos, about the son of a shipmate of Prentiss on the *Danube*.)

PRESCIADO, JOSE "MEXICAN JOE": Presciado (1843–unknown) was brought to the island around 1850 by the Frank Whittley family, who were shepherds in the hills above White's Landing. "Mexican Joe," who was born in Sonora, became known as the best boatman and hunting and fishing guide on the island.

PROHIBITION ERA: A favorite smuggling spot on Catalina in different eras was Salta Verde Point. During the 1920s, mules would haul the booze up Silver Canyon and over Divide Road. Men would take over at that point and surreptitiously carry the bottles into Avalon. Locals recalled that Slavic immigrants on Whittley and Marilla Avenues would enlist children to stomp grapes in their bathtubs to make wine. The area of those two streets became known as "Vinegar Hill" because of the odoriferous fermenting process used to make wine and whiskey. After the Twenty-first Amendment in 1933 cancelled the crime-generating Eighteenth Amendment to prohibit alcoholic beverages, the first Avalon business to successfully apply for a liquor license was Abe Perluss's store on Sumner Avenue. The store is known today as Abe's Liquor.

PROPST, ALLEN DOUGLAS: Doug Propst (December 1, 1926–November 4, 2003) was hired by the Santa Catalina Island Company in 1953 as a cowboy to supervise its cattle program. Propst managed the company herd, installed fences, built watering ponds and supervised land restoration projects. A native of Merino, Colorado, who had served in the navy during World War II, he received a bachelor's degree in animal husbandry from Colorado A&M University (today's Colorado State). He developed a deep appreciation for Catalina's potential and worked closely with P.K. Wrigley to develop the Catalina Island Conservancy in 1972. He was named president of the conservancy in 1975. On February 2, 1994, when Propst retired, a special dinner aboard the *Queen Mary* in Long Beach included many testimonials to his forty years of outstanding service to the island and its natural resources. On September 16, 1990, a profile written by Zan Thompson in the *Los Angeles Times* read, "It is gentling to the spirit to know there is such a place as the Catalina island high country and people like Doug Propst who hold it in trust for campers, hikers, riders, fishermen and just people who need to know such a place exists, just there, at the edge of the world."

Q

QUARRIES: The Tongva worked several soapstone (steatite) quarries for many millennia. Catalina's original rock quarry lies west of Long Point and Goat Harbor but east of Two Harbors. For the Tongva, steatite was a popular trading commodity with neighboring Channel Islands tribes and those on the mainland. Steatite was a soft, easily worked stone that had heat-tolerant qualities. Soapstone also was used for pipes and decorative or religious carvings. Powdered steatite was used to relieve chafing on babies under their arms and between their legs. In more recent times, quarrying was done under the watch of the sons of Phineas Banning, who bought the island in 1891 from the estate of James Lick and established the Santa Catalina Island Company to develop it as a resort. One motivation for the buy was to use Catalina's rocks to build a breakwater at Wilmington for the Banning shipping company. Prior to 1919, the rock was excavated between Empire Landing and Two Harbors. Later, the Graham Brothers, under contract with the Santa Catalina Island Company, managed this operation. The Pebbly Beach quarry, located at the East End of the island near Church Rock, is managed by the Connolly-Pacific Company, based in Long Beach. Catalina rock has built or shored up several breakwaters along the Southern California coast.

QUEEN CITY: The name of a town that never was, this moniker was intended for a settlement on the West End, west of the Isthmus. In 1863, on the West End, Fourth of July Harbor and Cherry Valley were home to as many as sixty speculators for precious metals. The following year, the Union army arrived and found that only three shanties had been erected on the abandoned town site.

R

RADIO: "From the beautiful Casino Ballroom, overlooking Avalon Bay at Catalina Island, we bring you the music of..." During the 1930s, live musical broadcasts were popular. P.K. Wrigley was a friend of Lew Atlas, president of the Columbia Broadcasting System (CBS), which had its main studios and offices in the Wrigley Building in Chicago. In 1934, Wrigley arranged for nightly broadcasts of dance music from the Casino Ballroom. Music from the ballroom was aired in two half-hour segments, from 9:30 to 10:00 p.m. and from 11:00 to 11:30 p.m. In Southern California, the music was heard over Los Angeles station KHJ-AM, a part of the CBS Pacific Coast System. Segments were also broadcast over the national CBS network. Airtime was not limited to dance music. The cross-channel Aquaplane Races were broadcast from the Casino over the Mutual Broadcasting System (MBS) in 1937. Beginning in 1939, *Kay*

The Leighton Noble Orchestra was just one of the many big bands to play the Avalon Casino in the mid-twentieth century. Some bands arrived around mid-June and stayed the entire summer season. Others came in early summer, played six weeks or so and then were replaced by season-closing bands. Some were led by Benny Goodman, Dick Jurgens, Kay Kyser, Freddy Martin and Bob Crosby. *Courtesy of Marvin Carlberg.*

Kyser's Kollege of Musical Knowledge, sponsored by the American Tobacco Company, was broadcast from the Avalon Theatre from 6:00 to 7:00 p.m. every Wednesday over NBC. Bandleaders such as Ben Bernie, Gary Breckner, Bob Crosby, Jan Garber and Ted Weems all advanced their national popularity by broadcasting from Catalina. During World War II, broadcasting from the Casino continued. The dedication ceremonies for the U.S. Maritime Services Training Center at Avalon were heard over MBS on December 15, 1942. Many USO shows from the Casino went out over CBS by way of KNX in Los Angeles and worldwide by the Armed Forces Radio Network as shortwave transmissions. In 1952, KBIG, with transmitters on the island, broadcast dance music locally at 740 on the AM dial. Today, the community of Avalon is served by an independent radio station, KISL.

EL RANCHO ESCONDIDO: Philip and Helen Wrigley established this 1,500-acre ranch in the 1930s on the windward side of the island to breed wild horses and then, two decades later, Arabian show horses. When the couple passed away in 1977, their children took over the ranch. The

Santa Catalina Island Company operates the ranch. Several wine grape varieties are grown there. The grapes are harvested and flown to Rusack Vineyards in Santa Barbara. Horses are no longer kept at the rancho. El Rancho Escondido Road connects the Airport in the Sky with Little and Shark Harbors.

RENTON, DAVID MALCOLM: "D.M." Renton (February 8, 1878–May 27, 1947) was a builder and business associate of William Wrigley Jr. His notable Catalina constructions include the Avalon Casino, Atwater Hotel, Wrigley's personal home at Mount Ada and the Thompson Reservoir. Wrigley and Renton had a great working relationship. Wrigley reportedly referred to Renton as his "hands." Together, Wrigley and Renton established the Catalina Clay Products at Pebbly Beach, which was sold in 1937 to the Gladding, McBean company. Tiles created from the original molds are popular collectors' items today. Renton's last construction project for the Wrigley family was the Wrigley Memorial. The plans used Catalina materials, flagstone and tiles. The memorial is open to the public at the Wrigley Memorial & Botanic Garden and is managed by the Catalina Island Conservancy. Renton was vice-president of the Santa Catalina Island Company until his 1936 retirement. His work was not just in Avalon; one of his solo efforts was the observation tower to house a sixty-inch telescope at the Mount Wilson Observatory.

RENTON MINE: A short-lived mine in the mid-1920s in the rugged hills behind Pebbly Beach generated ore, including silver, zinc and lead. Renton Mine Road is the official start (or end) of the 37.2-mile Trans-Catalina Trail, just east of Avalon.

REPTILES AND AMPHIBIANS: Native to Catalina are five snakes, three lizards, one salamander and a frog. The Santa Catalina side-blotched lizard is ubiquitous and often seen in gardens or on hiking trails. Additionally, two species of herpetofauna have been introduced to Catalina and qualify in conservation terms as exotic invaders: the red-eared slider and the bullfrog. The native southern Pacific rattlesnake, which can be three to four feet long, is the only venomous reptile on the island.

RIBBON BEACH: Located a little more than two miles southwest of the West End on the south side of the island, Ribbon Beach is accessible by boat only.

RIBBON ROCK: This dark, vertical rock wall contains a gigantic ribbon of quartz that is visible for many miles. It was formed twenty million years ago when lighter hot rocks were pushed through cracks in the darker bedrock by incredible volcanic forces. It is accessible from the water only, nearly three miles southeast of the West End.

Ribbon Rock, on the windward side of the island, is 2.9 miles southeast of the West End. This is a dark, vertical rock wall with a gigantic ribbon of quartz that can be seen from several miles out to sea. *Photo by Justin Peter.*

RIPPERS COVE: A boat-in campsite on the leeward side of the island, this inlet is located four miles east of Two Harbors and 8.6 miles west of Avalon. An offshore reef attracts snorkelers.

ROBBINS, TOMAS: Robbins (1801–July 15, 1854) petitioned the last Mexican governor of California, Pío Pico, to use the island as a ranch. Pico granted the island to him in 1846, two years before the Treaty of Guadalupe Hidalgo ceded Alta California to the United States. According to one undocumented story, the governor, an avid horseman who loved racing, accepted a white horse and silver saddle in return. This was the last Spanish or Mexican land grant in California and is credited as the reason Catalina is the only privately owned island of the Channel Islands today. Robbins had acquired, about the same time, some three thousand acres called Rancho Las Positas y La Calera in present-day Hope Ranch in Santa Barbara. A major north–south street in Santa Barbara carries the name Robbins.

S

SALTA VERDE POINT: Spanish for "green springs," Salta Verde Point is a favorite of scuba divers. Kelp forests are one hundred yards offshore, and the area teems with fish and other marine life. On the ridgeline above Salta Verde Point, Santa Verde Ridge Road is a two-and-a-half-mile dirt road running west from Coffee Pot Canyon and then north to Bullrush Canyon Road.

SANTA CATALINA ISLAND: Portuguese-born explorer Juan Rodríguez Cabrillo claimed the island for Spain on October 7, 1542, christening it San Salvador after his ship. Another Spanish explorer, Sebastián Vizcaíno, arrived on the island on November 24, 1602, the eve of Saint Catherine's Day, and he renamed the island in the saint's honor. It has been Santa Catalina ever since.

SANTA CATALINA ISLAND COMPANY: In 1892, William Banning claimed the deed for Catalina Island for $128,740 from the trustees of James Lick, after George Shatto, who had bought the island for $200,000 from Lick, was unable to keep up the mortgage payments. However, Shatto had created and subdivided the town of Avalon, providing Banning with a turnkey development with which to work. In 1896, Banning deeded the island to the Santa Catalina Island Company, which he had established two years earlier. The company was family owned, the stock held by three Banning brothers (William, Hancock and Joseph) and their two sisters (Katherine and Anna). The brothers went to work to develop the island into a pleasure resort. Over a span of twenty-three years, the Bannings built commuter roads throughout the island's interior, ran glass-bottomed boat tours and vigorously promoted sport fishing.

In 1913, Avalon was incorporated as Los Angeles County's thirtieth city. However, the great fire of 1915 put a hold on any more development. All progress came to a halt until 1918, when the Hotel St. Catherine was built and opened. Under the direction and ownership of William Wrigley Jr., in 1919 the Island Company once again revived its commitment to tourism by building the current Casino, Bird Park and golf course. More recently, it opened the Zip Line Eco Tour and refreshed Descanso Beach. The Santa Catalina Island Company is one of the largest employers on the island and manages many of the retail shops and restaurants in Avalon and Two Harbors. Through a partnership agreement with the Catalina Island Conservancy and the state, it manages interior and boat-in camping sites.

SANTA CATALINA ISLAND INCLINE RAILWAY: Also known as the Island Mountain Railway and Angels Flight (even though that was the name of a similar and more famous Los Angeles city tram), this was a scenic tourism draw on the south side of Avalon that ran up to Buena Vista Point, traveling between the old Greek Amphitheatre and the Holly Hill House. A teahouse provided refreshments at the top. A second tram ran on the south side of the hill, up from and down to Pebbly Beach. The funicular's popularity ended with the Avalon fire of 1915.

SCHOOLS: Avalon schools are in the Long Beach Unified School District. Four schools operate on Catalina Island. Two Harbors is served by a one-room schoolhouse for grades kindergarten through five. West End students travel to Avalon for grades six through twelve. Avalon schools are grouped on one campus, including Avalon Elementary School, Avalon Middle School and Avalon High School. Additionally, thousands of school-age youths travel from the mainland to study each year at one of the several camps on the island and through programs managed by the Catalina Island Conservancy.

SCUBA DIVING: During World War II, "frogmen" trainees of the Office of Strategic Services (OSS), based at Toyon Bay on the island's northern coast, experimented with "rebreather" apparatuses, which absorbed the carbon dioxide of the user's exhaled breath to permit the recycling of the substantially unused oxygen content of each breath. After the war, Catalina's crystal-clear waters beckoned divers. By then, the new self-contained underwater breathing apparatus (SCUBA) device invented by Émile Gagnan and Jacques-Yves Cousteau was gaining in popularity. The first formal scuba-training program started on Catalina in 1958, when diver John Hardy, a water safety instructor at YMCA's Camp Fox, began giving lessons. Hardy and other camp directors finally received official underwater instructor credentials in 1960. Scuba diving has been among Catalina's most popular activities and cottage industries ever since.

SEA MONSTER LEGEND: In the depths between Santa Catalina and San Clemente Islands, there supposedly swims a sea monster that dozens of people throughout the twentieth century have seen. The often-cited lengthy report on the always briefly glimpsed leviathan was printed in the June 1934 edition of *Esquire* under the byline of Ralph Bandini. "A great barrel shaped Thing," Bandini wrote, "tapering toward the top and surmounted by a reptilian head strangely resembling those of the huge, prehistoric creatures whose reproductions stand in various museums. It lifted what must have been a good twenty feet. Widely spaced in the head were two eyes—eyes such as were never conceived of even in the wildest nightmare! Immense, at least a full foot in diameter, round, slightly bulging, and as dead looking as though they had seen all the death the world has suffered since its birth! No wonder those who had seen it close by could speak of little else but the eyes!" A posthumous inductee into the International Game Fish Association Hall of Fame, Bandini was one of the scions of the noted Los Angeles Bandini family and a rather respected sportsman who had written *Veiled Horizon: Stories of Big Game Fish of the Sea*. He was a member of Avalon's prestigious Tuna Club.

In 1920, Captain George Farnsworth glimpsed the "monster" while out fishing. "Its eyes were 12 inches in diameter...it had a big mange of hair, about two feet long." In 1927, Howard Wilson, the Orange County editor of the *Los Angeles Times*, described the monster as brownish, with a camel-like head and neck with "eyes like dinner plates and a neck that extended some ten feet above the surface of the sea." A 1941 edition of *National Geographic* opined, "It is more than likely that there is a real 'sea serpent' [based on] many reports of a huge-bodied, long-necked creature, somewhat resembling the supposedly extinct plesiosaurus." In a case of life imitating mythology, in October 2013, a dead eighteen-foot oarfish was found off Catalina Island near Toyon Bay. Deepwater oarfish typically surface when they are sick or dying and have fueled tales of sea serpents worldwide.

SEAL ROCKS: Located at the extreme Eastern End of the island, Seal Rocks is a natural summertime habitat for migratory California sea lions and a favorite tourist attraction by boat.

SENTINEL ROCK: Located off the point between Ben Weston Beach and Cottonwood Beach on the island's windward side, this is a popular bird-watching site.

SHALER, WILLIAM: Shaler (1773–March 29, 1833) was a Yankee merchant who doubled as a government official as he commanded trading vessels sailing the California coast. His ship, the *Leila Byrd*, was anchored off the island from March 14 to May 1, 1804, for repairs. He named the natural harbor of his anchorage Port Roussillon, after a friend. Conventional thought put this sojourn at today's Avalon Bay, but some evidence points to the fact that it might have been at the Isthmus. In either case, Shaler was the first American to name a location on the island, even though the place is unconfirmed and the name didn't last. Shaler went on to become a political diplomat influencing the future growth of both the trade and boundaries of the United States. He wrote some 150 political letters between 1810 and 1813 for the administrations of James Madison and Andrew Jackson. In some ways, Shaler was ahead of his time. For instance, he envisioned a partnership with Great Britain to "create a new balance of power as a source of international stability." This was before the War of 1812, a thirty-two-month military conflict between the United States and Great Britain. In 1804, Shaler stopped short of advocating the annexation of California from New Spain, hinting only that "the conquest of this country would be absolutely nothing; it would fall without an effort to the most inconsiderable force." Eight years later, in August 1812, he still assumed that California would remain a foreign province, even after its Pacific trade came under the control of Great Britain following the collapse of Spain. Of course, California's gold rush was just around the corner, which eventually paid in large part for the arming of the Union in the Civil War.

SHARK HARBOR: A windward-side inlet divided from Little Harbor by the rock formation known as the Whale's Tail, this is a surfing destination when conditions are right. Although there might be sharks in the water, the site was given its name for a rock formation offshore that, depending on the tide, looks like a shark fin (a guano-covered shark fin) sticking out of the water.

SHATTO, GEORGE RUFUS: Shatto (August 15, 1850–May 31, 1893) purchased Catalina Island for $200,000 from the James Lick estate in 1887. He is credited with building the town's first hotel, the original Hotel Metropole, located between Metropole and Whittley Avenues. He built a pier and purchased the steamer *Ferndale* for regular cross-channel voyages during the summer months. He platted or laid out the streets and lots of Avalon, organizing the grid that exists today, and began the sale of residential lots. At the time of his purchase, the harbor was called Timms Landing after merchant Augustus Timms of San Pedro, California. The Catalina town was to be renamed Shatto's City. But his sister-in-law, Etta Marilla Whitney, suggested Avalon, a reference to Lord Alfred Tennyson's "Idylls of the King." Shatto sold the mining rights to Catalina to the International Mining Syndicate Ltd. of London, but that deal was erased in an English court. Eventually, Shatto couldn't keep up his payments to the Lick estate and sold the island to J.B. Banning for one dollar in 1891. Two years later, Shatto died at the age of thirty-two in a train accident just above Newhall, California. The *Reno Weekly Gazette and Stockman* reported on June 8 that the tragic news was broken to Mrs. Shatto by Reverend Dr. Campbell. "Mrs. Shatto gave a pitiable scream when she heard the news and fainted," the paper wrote. "She has been in a semi-unconscious condition all day and under the care of a physician."

Ship Rock is about three miles off the coast of Catalina's isthmus. Its pointed shape, covered with bird guano, causes it to look like a sailboat at full mast. *Photo by Justin Peter.*

SHEEP CHUTE: This four-mile-long service road transects the island from the Airport in the Sky to Little Harbor as a portion of the Trans-Catalina Trail.

SHIP ROCK: A rock in the ocean about a mile and a half north of the Isthmus resembles a masted sailing ship.

SILVER CANYON: The watershed just above Silver Canyon Landing on the windward side of the island's East End is often a resting spot for the island's bison. Silver Canyon Landing is a small, sandy beach on the windward side of the island's East End, just west of the Palisades.

SILVER PEAK: The highest point on the island's West End, this mountain rises 1,804 feet above sea level. Silver Peak Road is a service road that runs the length of the island's spine on the West End, connecting Catalina Harbor with Mile 36 of the Trans-Catalina Trail between Black Point and the trail's end at Starlight Beach.

SKULL RIDGE ROAD: This three-mile hiking road connects on either end with Middle Ranch Road.

SMUGGLING: Following the War of 1812, the Spanish occupational government in California closed every California port to all foreign vessels. Yankee traders unwilling to accept the sanctions began a lucrative and illegal smuggling operation that made full use of Catalina's coves and harbors. Smuggling was so intense and pervasive that the Spaniards were at a loss to regulate it. When Mexico took control of California, including Catalina, in 1820, trading of contraband continued. Tariffs were the Mexican government's only source of revenue. The tariffs, set at 100 percent of the value of the declared merchandise, were paid at the customhouse in Monterey. Ships would stop there, pay the tariff and then be free to trade along the coast. To avoid paying duty, skippers would unload the expensive merchandise at various coves around Catalina. A group of sailors would be left to guard the loot while the trading ship would head to Monterey to pay tariff on the diminished cargo of goods, then sail back to Catalina to pick up the undeclared merchandise.

When the Treaty of Guadalupe Hidalgo ceded Alta California to the United States in 1848, free trade was granted up and down the coast. However, in 1853, smugglers plied their trade once more, this time with human cargos of Chinese laborers brought over to help build the Transcontinental Railroad. China Point on the windward side of the island is a leftover moniker from the human-cargo era. Despite Prohibition, the *Catalina Islander* reported in 1923 that one thousand cases of whiskey were cached on the beach near Eagle Rock. The Channel Islands were used to stow illegal booze from Canada and Latin America, and stories too numerous to recall here of nighttime deliveries on beaches from Ventura County to Manhattan Beach to Anaheim Bay are testimony to the tenacity of the Prohibition-era rumrunners. The island's status as a contraband way station occasionally still makes the news. On May 18, 2011, the Los Angeles County Sheriff's Department spotted a man with big plastic-wrapped objects at remote Little Harbor during a routine patrol. The SWAT team was flown in, and the objects turned out to be thirty-one bales of marijuana weighing about 1,500 pounds and worth about $750,000.

SOAPSTONE: Outcroppings of soapstone or steatite were dug from the ground and used by the Native American Tongva to fashion heat-resistant, nearly shatterproof cooking pots and jugs. The industrious Tongva exported hand-sculpted utensils and effigies to the mainland, where tribes from Southern California to Oregon and Washington bartered for them. An easily visible, existing soapstone quarry can be viewed on the Soapstone Trail, part of the Airport Loop Trail that circles the Airport in the Sky.

SOUTHERN CALIFORNIA EDISON: The power giant's Pebbly Beach Generating Station in Avalon is a combination of electric generating station and liquefied petroleum gas distribution facility. The Pebbly Beach Generating

Station provides both electricity and gas for the entire island. Historically, diesel internal combustion engines created the island's electricity. In December 2011, twenty-three propane-powered Capstone C65 micro turbines were installed, replacing the diesel generators. Edison operates a gas pipeline distribution system serving the city of Avalon. Liquefied petroleum gas is stored and vaporized at Edison's Catalina Utilities Center Facility at Pebbly Beach and is eventually distributed through approximately six and a half miles of pipeline at a pressure of six pounds per square inch.

SPORT FISHING: Big game sport fishing is traced to 1898 and Charles Frederick Holder, a marine biologist, early conservationist and creator of the Tournament of Roses in Pasadena. Holder was a professor of zoology at Throop Polytechnic Institute in Pasadena, which became Caltech. From his first visit to Catalina, Holder was impressed by the beauty of the kelp beds and the variety of colorful fish and other aquatic life in the near-shore waters. Holder was horrified that men were taking tuna on heavy hand lines and hauling them aboard boats. Holder and five associates formed the Tuna Club to preserve big game fishing as a sport in which the skill of the angler and the boatman is matched against the native cunning and strength of the fish. Almost immediately, anglers flocked to Catalina to try fishing for giant tuna and other species without the advantage of hand lines.

Holder secured lasting fame in the annals of sport fishing by using a rod and six hundred feet of No. 21 line (with a breaking strength of only 42 pounds) to land a six-foot, four-inch tuna weighing 183 pounds. Membership to the Tuna Club included the ability to land a game fish of more than 100 pounds using fishing line that the fish could actually break. Members of the Tuna Club included: Theodore Roosevelt, Herbert Hoover, Winston Churchill, General George S. Patton, Hal Roach, Cecil B. De Mille, Charlie Chaplin, Bing Crosby and noted western author and adventurer Zane Grey. The original Tuna Club building was built in 1908 and was destroyed in the great fire of 1915. The building was replaced and stands on the original location overlooking Avalon Harbor.

SPOUTING CAVE: Tides create a spray at this locale, near Blue Cavern Point east of the Isthmus.

SPRING LANDING: This small beach is located about two and a quarter miles east of Land's End on the windward side of the West End.

STAGECOACH ROAD: Begun on March 20, 1897, and completed on June 1, 1898, this route through the island's rugged interior finally connected

After acquiring the island from George Shatto, the Banning brothers proceeded to construct commuter roads through the island's interior. This view of the Stagecoach Road looks east toward Avalon from the summit. *Courtesy of Marvin Carlberg.*

In 1908, coach excursions were a popular attraction for visitors to Catalina. The views from the precipitous Stagecoach Road up out of Avalon are as breathtaking today as they were then. *Courtesy of Marvin Carlberg.*

Avalon and Two Harbors with an overland road. Engineered by Samuel S. Farnsworth and financed by the Banning Company, it was built with picks and shovels. The twenty-three-mile, horse-drawn trip included a steep, three-mile ascent out of Avalon and took two days to complete. By 1914, automobiles had begun traveling the route, and it was widened at spots. Today, the mostly paved road—also known as Stage Coach Road and Stage Road—remains the main cross-island route, traversing rugged and scenic landscapes.

STAR BAY: This small beach is located about a mile and a half east of Land's End on the windward side of the West End.

STARLIGHT BEACH: The official beginning or end of the 37.2-mile Trans-Catalina Trail is at this beach on the leeward side of the far West End.

STRATTON-PORTER, GENEVA OR "GENE": Stratton-Porter (August 17, 1863–December 6, 1924) was an accomplished American author and one of the earliest women to form a movie studio and production company, the Gene Stratton-Porter Film Company. Estimates at one time put her readership at fifty million. Her novel *A Girl of the Limberlost* was adapted on four occasions by filmmakers, most recently in 1990 for television. Eight of Stratton-Porter's twelve novels were also adapted for film. In 1921, she worked with Thomas Ince to film *Michael O'Halloran*. Although she had gained considerable fame and recognition, her wealth allowed her to do that which she loved the most: explore and write about natural history. Despite not finishing high school, she became a lifelong scholar specializing in ecology and wildlife. She developed skills as an amateur naturalist and wildlife photographer, excelling at images of birds and moths. She also published a number of nature books but was rarely recognized for her contributions to science. She used her fame and income to conserve Limberlost Swamp, one of the last of the wetlands of the lower Great Lakes Basin. The wetlands in Indiana were the inspiration for her namesake novel, *A Girl of the Limberlost*. She owned five acres on Catalina Island and built a home in Avalon on Catalina Street; it is now the Singing Water Christian Center at 346 Catalina Avenue. Of her Catalina home, she wrote, "On the mountain I am going to set my workshop, fashioned much like Limberlost Cabin in size and arrangement, but differing from it in architecture, as it must to conform to this location; and around it I am going to begin growing the wild flowers of California. I want it, also, as I want any spot on which I live, to become a sanctuary for the birds."

SUGARLOAF: A rock formation existed at the spot where the Casino stands today. The giant boulder onshore was called Big Sugarloaf, and the small

The home of popular 1920s novelist Gene Stratton-Porter was located on a double lot at 346 Catalina Avenue, now the site of the Catalina Bible Church. She intended it to be her vacation hideaway, but she never lived there. She left Avalon for a book-signing tour in 1924 and was killed on December 6 in an automobile accident in Los Angeles. She was fifty-six. *Courtesy of Marvin Carlberg*

This 1905 view of Little Sugarloaf Rock shows the precarious wooden steps up to an observation deck on top. Little Sugarloaf was dynamited away so that it wouldn't block the view of the Casino. *Courtesy of Marvin Carlberg*

offshore boulder was called Little Sugarloaf—also occasionally referenced as "Sugar Loaf." To build the first casino, Sugarloaf Casino, or the little or first Casino, Big Sugarloaf was dynamited out of existence and shoved into the bay between where it once stood and Little Sugarloaf, creating most of Casino Point. William Wrigley Jr. wanted to keep Little Sugarloaf when he decided to build the new, bigger Casino. But it was evident that Little Sugarloaf would partially block the view of the new Casino, being erected in 1929. Little Sugarloaf, too, was obliterated by dynamite. The Sugarloaf or little Casino was removed to become part of the Bird Park in Avalon Canyon. An attraction of old Little Sugarloaf was a precarious set of wooden steps up to an observation deck on top.

SUMNER STREET: Charles A. Sumner was the assistant manager of George Shatto's holdings and, as such, was the first manager of the Hotel Metropole in 1887.

SWAIN'S CANYON: This watershed on the leeward side of the island descends down from Airport Road to Toyon Bay. Lawson Swain, aka Swain Lawson, occasionally referenced as "Swaine" or "Swayne," was an early island resident.

SWEETWATER CANYON: This small watershed collects the runoff south of Mount Banning and Mount Orizaba.

T

THOMPSON RESERVOIR: Also known today as Middle Ranch Reservoir, this man-made lake is the primary gauge that the municipality of Avalon uses to evaluate freshwater availability for Avalon. Several sixty-five-foot-deep wells tap the aquifer below the reservoir.

TOYON BAY: Located on the leeward side of the East End, this locale was the site of the exclusive Catalina Island School for Boys in the early 1900s. During World War II, the facility was turned into an Office of Strategic Services (OSS) training camp. Chinese and American men were trained in guerrilla warfare for use behind Japanese lines in China. After the war, Toyon Bay saw time as a boarding school and a singing camp and resort in the 1950s. The site was abandoned for two decades. In 1979, Guided Discoveries Inc. bought it and has since run the Catalina Island Marine Institute (CIMI), a science facility for children and summer campers. The name is derived from the Southern California native Toyon tree, also

Toyon Bay is the home of the Catalina Island Marine Institute (CIMI). It formerly was the Catalina Island School for Boys. In World War II, Toyon Bay served as a training headquarters of the Office of Strategic Services, the forerunner of the Central Intelligence Agency. *Photo by Justin Peter.*

known as Christmas berry. The berries resemble the red berries seen on holly. The same Toyon tree, native to arid Southern California hills, is responsible for the naming of Hollywood, California.

TRANS-CATALINA TRAIL: The 37.2-mile hiking course from Renton Mine Road on the East End to Starlight Beach on the West End was created by the Catalina Island Conservancy and dedicated in 2009.

TRASK, BLANCHE: Trask (July 26, 1865–November 11, 1916) was a rather famous island explorer, field botanist, poet, natural history essayist and *Los Angeles Times* contributor. From her homes at Big Fisherman's Cove and Avalon, Trask traversed the island on plant-hunting missions with a zeal matched by few. Reportedly, her husband filed for divorce because she "deserted" him. The story goes that she was a naturalist in more ways than one, deserting her wardrobe on botanic quests into the wild lands. This is undocumented, however.

Trask was born Luella Blanche Engle in Waterloo, Iowa, and died of pulmonary problems in November 1916. In the intervening years, her botanic treks covered all of the California Channel Islands, and at least seven plants of these isles carry her name. She published her notes on the floras of Santa Catalina and San Clemente islands in 1899 and 1904. Her friend and fellow botanist Willis Jepson wrote in his field notebook during her funeral in San Francisco, "Mrs. Trask was as [botanist] Miss [Alice] Eastwood expressed it, 'a wild woman'…and [in my mind] I saw Mrs. Trask, once again, on a high ridge beyond Avalon standing in the moonlit shadows far in the night in silent worship of the sea and air, completely controlled by love of strange beauty and mysticism."

TRAVILLA, WILLIAM: Travilla (March 22, 1920–November 2, 1990) was a costume designer for theater, films and television who was born on Catalina Island. Travilla was his professional name. He won an Academy Award in 1949 for his work on the *Adventures of Don Juan* but was perhaps best known for dressing Marilyn Monroe in eight of her films. She reportedly was so enamored with Travilla that she once autographed one of her famous calendars with the inscription: "Oh Billy dear please dress me forever, Love Marilyn." The pleated ivory cocktail dress Monroe wore in the 1955 film *The Seven Year Itch* was also one of Travilla's creations. It was included in an estate auction by Julien's in 2013 with an initial bid range of $20,000 to $30,000.

TUNA CLUB: The world's oldest sport fishing club was founded at Avalon in 1898 by conservationist Charles F. Holder and friends H.K. Macomber, E.L. Doran, C.R. Scudder and Fitch Dewery. Their purpose was to advocate against wasteful overfishing and for "a sport in which the skill… of the angler and the boatman is matched against the native cunning and strength of the fish." Holding its first meetings at the Hotel Metropole in Avalon, the Tuna Club gained two hundred members in eighteen months. Eventually, its ranks included Charlie Chaplin, Bing Crosby, Cecil B. DeMille, Zane Grey, Stan Laurel, Hal Roach, Theodore Roosevelt, Herbert Hoover, George S. Patton Jr. and William Wrigley Jr.

TWIN ROCKS: A point on the leeward side of the island between Goat Harbor and Italian Gardens, this has been the site of an active bald eagle nest.

TWO HARBORS: Known as "the Isthmus," this small, unincorporated village has a summer population of fewer than 500, and about 150 people live here year round. It is mainly a resort community containing a restaurant, hotel and general store. Notable features are a former Union Civil War barracks, one of only three such remaining buildings in California, and a one-room schoolhouse still in use. In the 1860s, mining operations for silver, lead and zinc took place in the area. In 1864, during the Civil War, the Union army sent eighty-three soldiers with camels and horses to the island to establish Camp Santa Catalina Island. They were to protect the area from Confederate privateers and survey the Isthmus and adjacent Catalina Harbor for the Bureau of Indian Affairs. The idea was to convert the island to a reservation for "militant" tribes. However, the reservation idea and camp were abandoned.

The barracks that the army built on the Isthmus was used in the 1920s and '30s to house visiting film crews and by the U.S. Coast Guard during World War II. In 1951, it became the home of the current Isthmus Yacht Club. A half mile from the barracks is where the *Ning Po* eventually burned. This Chinese merchant ship was built in 1753 and was involved in more than a century of war, rebellion and piracy, eventually finding its way to Catalina, where it was converted into a tourist attraction in 1913 at Pebbly Beach. It eventually made it over to Cat Harbor, where a fire destroyed it and also claimed several wooden sailing vessels, including the famous old down-easter *Llewellyn J. Morse*, which stood in for the USS *Constitution* in the silent film *Old Ironsides* (1926).

U

USC CATALINA HYPERBARIC CHAMBER: An important resource for sport divers and all scuba divers, this is a twenty-four-hour, seven-day-a-week emergency recompression facility at the University of Southern California's Wrigley Institute for Environmental Studies at Big Fisherman's Cove. The chamber has served and saved thousands of divers who frequent the waters of Southern California.

USC WRIGLEY INSTITUTE FOR ENVIRONMENTAL STUDIES (WIES): The University of Southern California's hub for environmental research, education and outreach, WIES is located in Big Fisherman's Cove near Two Harbors. The main offices are located in Los Angeles on USC's University Park campus, where staff oversees the research laboratories and conference facilities at the Philip K. Wrigley Marine Science Center. The faculty at the Wrigley Institute conducts research in all aspects of the environment, such as biological adaptations to climate change, interactions among humans and natural systems and the analysis and development of environmental policy. WIES works with foundations and the public to enhance environmental awareness. The Big Fisherman's Cove facilities include a three-thousand-square-foot laboratory building, dormitory housing, a cafeteria, a hyperbaric chamber and a large waterfront staging area complete with dock, pier, helipad and diving lockers. The facility was made possible by a donation from the Wrigley family in 1965.

UPPER BUFFALO RESERVOIR: This water source is located just to the southwest of Empire Landing.

V

VALLEY OF OLLAS: Located along the leeward side of the island, this canyon's mouth is at Rippers Cove. Translated from the Spanish, *ollas* means "pots." Tongva Native Americans who lived on the island for millennia crafted pots from the isle's soapstone.

VALLEY OF THE MOONS: An eroded watershed on the windward side of the East End, this canyon is located just below Coffee Pot Canyon.

VIZCAÍNO, SEBASTIÁN: Vizcaíno (1548–1624) was an established merchant in the trade between Mexico and Asia. In 1599, the viceroy of New Spain selected Vizcaíno to lead an expedition to explore the California coast. The objective was to find a port of call. This would confirm Spanish claims to the area and provide a place where the viceroyalty's ships could stop for repairs. Vizcaíno was to collect detailed information about weather, shoreline features, water depth and other resources. His maps were so accurate that they were used until 1790. He renamed the island from San Salvador—the name given by explorer Juan Rodriguez Cabrillo some sixty years prior—to Santa Catalina, in honor of the feast day of Saint Catherine of Alexandria on November 25, 1602.

W

WATER: In 1991, Avalon became the first city in California to flip the switch on a reverse osmosis plant that turns salty ocean water into drinking water. The plant cost $3 million to build and was a partial solution to a five-year drought that had reduced the Thompson Reservoir by 25 percent. The plant continues to augment the freshwater system originally built by William Wrigley Jr. as needed. The first recorded information about water on Catalina came from the historian on Vizcaíno's voyage. He wrote of the inhabitants of "Santa Catarina," who provided them with water "in a sort of bottle made of rushes." Frank LeCouvreur, who worked as a ranch hand in the summer of 1856, wrote that "the attractiveness [of the island] would certainly be great were not the absolute lack of fresh well water a material drawback for visitors or settlers…The necessary drinking water for a man and beast is drawn from cisterns and is decidedly disagreeable to the newcomer on account of its salty taste."

A half dozen or more of Catalina's springs and creeks do not dry up during the summer, but clean, fresh water continues to be a challenge. The Banning brothers planned on drilling a well in Avalon that was to care for the community's freshwater needs. It was absolutely necessary to have an abundant freshwater source to complete their ambitious plans to turn the island into a resort. They were unsuccessful and resorted to shipping fresh water to the town by barge. Locals recall taking saltwater baths during this time to conserve the fresh water. When William Wrigley Jr. took controlling interest in the Santa Catalina Island Company in 1919, he again looked in earnest for a freshwater solution that would support the fledgling resort. Water development culminated in 1924 in the construction of a 100-million-gallon reservoir, contained by the Thompson Dam. Several deep wells pull water from the aquifer below Thompson Reservoir. Twelve miles of pipeline enhanced with pumps at strategic locations move the water over a 1,460-foot peak to the Wrigley Reservoir. From there, it is gravity fed to Avalon below.

WATER TANK ROAD: This three-mile dirt hiking road on the West End runs north from the 28.5-mile marker on the Silver Peak Trail to the West End Road at Howland's Landing.

WELLS BEACH: Located on the western side of Catalina Harbor at the Isthmus, Wells Beach is the trailhead for the Silver Peak Road, a very steep, 3.0-mile dirt hiking road and a leg of the 37.2-mile Trans-Catalina Trail.

WEST END: The far western portion of the island, from Two Harbors to the point at Land's End, is generally known by this collective name. The West End includes the coves at Howland's and Parsons' Landings, Emerald Bay and, on the windward side, Lobster Bay. West End Road traverses the area, and West End Bison Corral is located there.

WESTON, BENJAMIN: Weston was a farmer and rancher in the area that became the Los Angeles County South Bay cities of Lomita and Torrance. He partnered with Nathaniel Narbonne in the nineteenth century to raise wheat and sheep on Catalina. The remnants of an old stone structure on the beach that bears his name (see Ben Weston Beach) on the windward side of the island was said to be his "cabin."

WEST POINT: This peak at the extreme West End has an elevation of 673 feet.

WHALE ROCK: This rocky outcropping on the windward side of the West End forms a lagoon between Ribbon Rock and Kelp Point.

WHALE'S TAIL: This large, natural rock formation, resembling its name, separates Shark Harbor from Little Harbor on the windward side of the island.

WHITE'S LANDING: This is the widest sand beach on the island. Thousands of years ago, it was a large Tongva village. White's Landing was also the home of Swayne Lawson, who came to Catalina in 1862 and lived in a cave with only a few goats he tamed for companions. In the 1920s, Mount Black Jack, rising 2,010 feet above White's Landing, generated ore for a short time. An aerial track carried ore to a barge that was towed down to the somewhat ponderously named Silver Isle 100 Ton Flotation Mill. Silver, zinc and lead were extracted there for about two years. Five hundred cloth sacks were filled with 150 pounds each of zinc concentrate and were shipped directly to Belgium every two weeks. All ore from Renton and Black Jack Mines was processed at this mill during the 1920s. White's Landing has been home to the Balboa Yacht Club since 1957 and the Catalina Experience, a youth and family camp.

WHITTLEY'S PEAK: This mountain has an elevation of 1,302 feet above sea level and is located on the leeward side of the East End. It's named for one of the early Catalina sheep and cattle ranchers, Frank P. Whittley, who built the old Catalina Country Club in 1888. Whittley Avenue in Avalon was also named for Whittley.

WILD BOAR GULLEY: Doug Propst, a ranch manager for the Wrigley family in the 1950s and the first president of the Catalina Island Conservancy, often drove botanists around the island to aid their collections. Robert Thorne and Percy Everett were two of them. Propst rediscovered the long-missing Catalina mountain mahogany (*Cercocarpus traskiae*) in what Thorne named Wild Boar Gully on the south side of the East End. That was in honor of a feral pig that, as Thorne said, "tried to hook me with his tusks as he charged out of the bushes and down the gully." Thorne, who revised *The Flora of Catalina* and was director of the Rancho Santa Ana Botanic Garden, also recalled, "Doug, safely ensconced in one of the larger mahogany trees, was much amused as I leapt over the gully."

WILLOW COVE: This boat-in campground on the leeward side of the island is located directly to the west of Toyon Bay.

Windle, Judge Ernest: Windle (March 16, 1879–February 12, 1968) came to Catalina Island by accident in 1907 to die. He had been working in a shipyard in Wilmington when a sling ship broke on a wharf and buried him under lumber. Broken bones and internal injuries led physicians to believe his days were numbered, so they sent him to Catalina. He did die on Catalina, but many years later, one month shy of ninety. In the years between, he founded and published the *Catalina Islander* newspaper, served as a judge and wrote and published books on philosophy. The *Catalina Islander*, which began publishing in 1913, remains a tradition today as the second-oldest regularly published newspaper in California, after the *Los Angeles Times*. For its twenty-fifth anniversary in December 1938, resident W.J. Laurin lauded Windle's editorial leadership by writing, "There have been no scare headlines, no lurid 'murder or divorce scandal' scoops: if it wasn't clean or constructive it wasn't fit to print in the *Islander*. Such has been the editorial policy of the publisher, Judge Ernest Windle. No newspaper or editor can set a higher ideal and for a quarter of a century live up to it."

Windle presided over the island's legal issues as magistrate for five decades starting in 1917 and was one of the nation's longest-seated judges. His obituary in the *Fresno Bee* reported that he had heard fourteen thousand cases, married more than 1,100 couples and once imposed a five-dollar fine on actor Errol Flynn for not having his dog on a leash. The reported story is that Flynn's unleashed dog attacked Windle's on the pier. Challenged by the judge, Flynn is supposed to have retorted: "I'm Errol Flynn and I don't have to have my dog on leash." Identifying himself as the judge, Windle replied, "Court's in session, and you're fined $5." The fine was suspended when Flynn apologized. The Catalina Islander Press published Windle's book *Exploring the Psychic Mind (Salvaging Human Emotions, Conquest of Fear, Humor & Human Mind, Stimulants on Human Emotions, Breathing, etc.)* in February 1939. The book was the culmination of years of columns on motivation and breathing. He also published a history of Catalina in 1931 and updated it twice. He wrote and published *Man and His Motives* with James Windle in 1954. He is interred in the Avalon Cemetery, and a memorial plaque is dedicated in his honor under a tree by the public library.

Windward Beaches: This collective name covers the swimming, camping and picnicking areas on the island's southwestern coast, particularly Ben Weston Beach, Cottonwood Beach and the contiguous Shark and Little Harbors.

A catamaran makes its way along the coast of Catalina Island. The remote windward side of the island contains such picturesque spots at Salta Verde Point, Cottonwood Beach, the adjacent Little and Shark Harbors and Catalina Harbor. *Photo by Justin Peter.*

WORLD WAR I: World War I had little effect on Catalina Island, save for the fact that it coincided with the great fire of 1915, which destroyed much of Avalon, bringing commerce to a standstill. The United States Maritime Service took over the island. However, on Avalon Canyon Drive, near where the Chicago Cubs conducted spring training from 1921 to 1951, is a weathered stone tower affixed with a copper plaque with a message from William Wrigley Jr. The plaque reads, "This tower was erected by Wm. Wrigley, Jr., in honor of the baseball players who gave or risked their lives in the defense of their country in the great world war. Jan. 15, 1926."

WORLD WAR II: With the advent of the Second World War, Catalina Island was the first line of defense for the nation's West Coast. Immediately after the bombing at Pearl Harbor, P.K. Wrigley, the son of William Wrigley Jr., leased the island to the United States government for the sum of one dollar. Sun-drenched Avalon, already famous as a destination for movie stars and celebrities, became a federal military zone. Both the SS *Catalina* and the SS *Cabrillo*, which carried tourists to Avalon and back, adopted new roles as transport ships, carrying military and wartime workers across San Francisco Bay. Even the *Blanche W*, a flying fish excursion boat named after William Wrigley Jr.'s granddaughter Ada Blanche Wrigley, was pressed into service in San Francisco Bay. The SS *Avalon* was also "drafted" into the war effort to carry military and civilian passengers between the island and the mainland.

Tourism was halted, causing Catalina's economy to tank. Many residents left the island for the duration of the war because on the mainland they could find work. Wrigley and others came up with a plan to provide island jobs by getting boat fuel to commercial fishermen who were contracted to fish for albacore tuna. The tuna fed both the civilian and military population on the island. With tourism off the table, the hundreds of hotel rooms, including those at the posh Hotel St. Catherine in Descanso Canyon, were turned into barracks. The entire island was retooled as a training ground for the military. The largest military contingency on the island was the United States Maritime Service. From 1942 to 1945, tens of thousands of young men trained for service on Liberty Ships that acted as a supply line to the two battlefronts in the Pacific and Europe. At Two Harbors, the U.S. Coast Guard trained its recruits. They practiced their seamanship on small boats in Isthmus Harbor. The country's top-secret Office of Strategic Services (OSS), the forerunner to the Central Intelligence Agency, trained for assignments behind enemy lines at Toyon Bay, Howland's Landing and Fourth of July Cove. Commandos training on Catalina had access to state-of-the-art weapons and explosives. Nicknamed "Bang Bang Boys," the trainees were each subjected to a five-day survival experience in the island's rugged interior with only a knife and fishing line. Another exercise was to enter Avalon by water, using experimental scuba gear. The goal was to "capture" a town landmark such as the bank or post office by placing an identifiable mark on the prize. What made this exercise particularly dangerous was that armed military guards were on watch in the harbor. Any OSS commando who was spotted stood the distinct possibility of being shot.

The only military installation on Catalina that was not primarily a training ground was the U.S. Army Signal Corps' Camp Cactus. Hidden by steep hills near Bullrush Canyon on the windward side of the island, Camp Cactus employed the first radar technology in the United States to detect enemy ships and aircraft approaching from the west. Antiaircraft guns were at the ready atop the island's steep cliffs. On the leeward side of the island, more defenses were installed at the new runway for the Buffalo Springs Airport, known today as the Airport in the Sky, ten miles from Avalon. When war broke out in 1941, construction on the

Upper Terrace Road leads to the Wrigleys' former home, which became the Inn at Mount Ada. *Photo by Justin Peter.*

runway was halted. Rocks, limbs, barbed wire and other obstacles were placed on the runway to thwart enemy aircraft from landing. The three-thousand-foot runway was completed and operational in 1946, the year after the war ended.

WRIGLEY, ADA ELIZABETH FOOTE: Ada (July 2, 1868–December 16, 1958) was the wife of William Wrigley Jr. Her husband tells the story of the first time he and Ada visited Catalina. Ada had gotten up early in the morning and was looking out the window when she called excitedly, "I should like to live here!" Wrigley joined her at the window and exclaimed, "I have never seen such a beautiful spot!" Shortly after that, the Wrigleys bought out all other investors and gained the controlling interest in Catalina Island.

WRIGLEY MEMORIAL & BOTANIC GARDEN: Named after William Wrigley Jr., this giant tribute to Catalina's great twentieth-century benefactor is at the top of Avalon Canyon. The imposing, 180-foot-high mausoleum continues memorializing Catalina's great booster, who was entombed there in 1933 until World War II. Before his remains were moved to Forest Lawn Cemetery in Glendale, California, the chewing gum tycoon's wife added a horticultural flourish. In 1935, Ada Wrigley enlisted the renowned Pasadena horticulturalist Albert Conrad to cultivate her private desert plant collection in the canyon below the memorial. With the war, maintenance ceased at the garden, which also languished through Ada Wrigley's death in 1959. Native and nonnative plants tangled and strangled the desert plant collection. In 1970, Malcolm Renton, executive director of the Santa Catalina Island Company, hired Catalina native and Huntington Beach nursery owner Mark Hoefs to remake the garden at the request of P.K. and Helen Wrigley. The Wrigley Memorial Foundation was formed in 1995 to oversee the thirty-eight acres, which are now a botanical attraction operated by the Catalina Island Conservancy. The garden contains many of Catalina's rare endemic and endangered plants.

WRIGLEY, PHILIP KNIGHT: Wrigley (December 5, 1894–April 12, 1977) was also known as "P.K." on the island but preferred to be called Phil. He was the son of William Wrigley Jr. and the successive leader of the family's enterprises after his father's death. While his father was known to be outgoing and charismatic, Phil's personality was more reserved and private. Despite beginning his leadership of the family company around the start of the Great Depression, Phil successfully led his company into generating a profit. P.K. inherited more than a successful business from his father; he also found himself the owner of Catalina Island and the Chicago Cubs. He took his responsibilities seriously with a sentimental interest in the Cubs. "The club and the park stand as memorials to my father," Phil said. "I will never dispose of my holdings in the club as long as the chewing gum business remains profitable enough to retain it." Like his father, Phil also loved Catalina Island and wanted to do what he could to protect it. Several biographers have quoted him as saying, "There is to be nothing of the Coney Island flavor about Santa Catalina." So on February 15, 1975, Phil Wrigley, with his wife, Helen, and his sister, Dorothy Wrigley Offield, deeded 88 percent of the island to the Catalina Island Conservancy, a nonprofit organization, to preserve and restore the isle's ecological health in perpetuity.

WRIGLEY, WILLIAM, JR.: Wrigley (September 3, 1861–January 26, 1932) was an entrepreneur who made his fortune by becoming the world's leading manufacturer of chewing gum and, in 1919, the largest stakeholder of the Santa Catalina Island Company. William began his career as a soap salesman for his father's business. After a few years, Wrigley was ready to branch out and start his own business. He arrived in Chicago with only thirty-two dollars in his pocket. To attract customers, William would give premiums with the purchase of his products. Soap came with two pieces of chewing gum with every purchase. He soon noticed that his patrons were more interested in the gum than the goods themselves, and so he decided to switch to selling gum. He went on to create the world's largest chewing gum manufacturing and distribution company. Juicy Fruit and Doublemint were two of his more recognizable product lines. He never forgot his beginnings and set the tone for the company by constantly telling his son Philip, "We are a five-cent business, and nobody in this company can ever afford to forget it."

In 1919, four years after the end of World War I, Wrigley Jr. entered a group investment venture to purchase Santa Catalina Island. Prior to the investment, Wrigley Jr. had never been to the island. He was persuaded to participate in the venture based on a single postcard. Upon visiting Catalina Island for the first time, Wrigley and his wife fell in love with the beauty of it and bought out his venture partners' shares, making him the majority shareholder. "This island business is much like providing for a big family," Wrigley said. "You first have to provide for the necessities before you go in for the trimmings and luxuries." That he did. He quickly set out to create much-needed infrastructure by laying roads, building a water reservoir and installing the largest diesel generator in California.

William and Ada Wrigley's one-time hilltop home in Avalon became a bed-and-breakfast. *Photo by Justin Peter.*

He promoted the island endlessly through advertising and sponsorship of such events as a cross-channel swim. As owner of the Chicago Cubs, he brought the team to the island for spring training. A tribute printed on July 11, 1935, in the *Catalina Islander* read, "He was a builder, planning and executing not for profit but for a social gain; these were given a spiritual unity through his attitude toward life."

γ

YACHT CLUBS: The beginning of Catalina's yacht clubs occurred when big game fishermen organized the Sophia Yacht Club (SYC) in 1903. The club was founded and dedicated by J.C. Tutt of Denver, the father of Sophia Tutt, who died while on a visit to Avalon in 1902. A foundation was constructed, and shafts were sunk overlooking Avalon Bay. But money ran out. The partially built foundation sat idle until J.E. "Pard" Matthewson, the glass-bottomed boat entrepreneur, erected a shop there to build his boat. The great fire of 1915 razed the shop. Years later, Art Sanger and his sister,

This view overlooks Avalon Harbor filled with boats during the summer months. More than four hundred moorings are available. The Holly Hill House is seen in the lower right corner from this vantage point on Mount Ada. *Photo by Justin Peter.*

Agnes Mondon, decided to turn the charred remains into a boathouse with a docking facility. Sanger and Mondon worked out an arrangement with the idle Sophia Yacht Club that allowed use of the facilities during the winter season. With the addition of several larger boats to the fleet, the name of the SYC changed in 1912 to the Catalina Motorboat Club. Taking over the site in 1924 was the Catalina Island Yacht Club. The building is quite distinctive with its functioning lighthouse motif. Other Yacht Clubs have since found a second home on Catalina and maintain facilities on the island.

YOUNG, GEORGE: Young (1910–August 6, 1972) was the first person documented to successfully swim the channel between Catalina Island and the mainland on January 15–16, 1927. He was participating in a contest called the Wrigley Ocean Marathon, sponsored by William Wrigley Jr. Young completed the twenty-two-mile swim in fifteen hours and forty-four minutes. The Canadian marathon swimmer was honored with the nickname the "Catalina Kid" and was awarded a prize of $25,000. In 1955, he was inducted into Canada's Sports Hall of Fame.

Bathing beauty "aquanauts" try an early version of water skiing. This was, no doubt, an event staged by the Hotel St. Catherine, built by the Bannings after the great Avalon fire of 1915. This photo dates back to no earlier than 1929, when the Casino, seen in the background, was constructed under the direction of William Wrigley Jr. *Courtesy of Marvin Carlberg*

Z

ZANE GREY PUEBLO: The namesake author of westerns built this rambling, four-level Pueblo Native American–style home (emulating Zuni and Hopi architecture) overlooking Avalon Bay on Avalon's northern hillside in 1924. Today, the building is a hotel.

BIBLIOGRAPHY

Primary Catalina Sources

Baker, Gayle, PhD. *Catalina Island: A Harbor Town History*. Santa Barbara, CA: Pacific Books, 2002.

Belanger, Joe. *Catalina Island: All You Need to Know*. Mesa, AZ: Roundtable Publishing, 2000.

Coates, Carole. *Catalina Island Pottery and Tile Treasures, 1927–1937*. Atglen, PA: Schiffer Publishing Ltd., 2012.

Doran, Adelaide LeMert. *The Ranch That Was Robbins': Santa Catalina Island*. Glendale, CA: Arthur H. Clark Company, 1964.

Fridley, A.W. *Catalina Pottery*. Long Beach, CA: Rainbow Publishing, 1977.

Gregg, Adelaide Le Mert. *A History of Santa Catalina Island from 1542 to 1919*. Los Angeles: Department of History, University of Southern California, 1934.

Greirson, Elizabeth. *"Hi, Naybor!" The Story of the Duke of Catalina*. Unspecified and undated, after 1977.

Grey, Zane. *Great Game Fishing at Catalina*. Avalon, CA: Santa Catalina Island Company, 1919.

Harris, Larry. *The Jewels of Avalon: Decorative Tiles of Catalina Island*. Avalon, CA: Catalina Jewels Publishing Company, 2002.

Heckman, Marlin L. *Santa Catalina Island in Vintage Postcards*. Charleston, SC: Arcadia Publishing, 2001.

Hein, Frank J., and Carlos L. de la Rosa. *Wild Catalina: Natural Secrets and Ecological Triumphs*. Charleston, SC: The History Press, 2013.

Hoefs, Steven, and Aisha Hoefs. *Catalina Island Pottery: Collectors Guide*. N.p.: S. & A. Hoefs, 1993.

BIBLIOGRAPHY

Holder, Charles Frederick. *An Isle of Summer, Santa Catalina: Its History, Climate, Sports, and Antiquities.* Los Angeles: R.Y. McBride, 1901.

Johnston, David L. *The Knights of Avalon: Seaplanes of Catalina.* Avalon, CA: Channel Catalina, 2005.

Kedis, Sherry, ed. *Catalina's Really Cookin': A Historical, Pictorial Cookbook.* Avalon, CA: Avalon Awareness Council, Avalon Schools Booster Club, n.d.

Mallan, Chicki, with Oz Mallan. *Guide to Catalina and California's Channel Islands.* 5th ed. Paradise, CA: Pine Press, 1996.

Martin, Terrence D., and Jeff Gnass. *Santa Catalina Island: The Story Behind the Scenery.* Wickenburg, AZ: KC Publications, 2003. [Initially published as *Santa Catalina Island: An Island Adventure* in 1984.]

McGroarty, John S. *California, Its History and Romance.* Los Angeles: Grafton Publishing Company, 1911.

McIntyre, Judy. *The Lore of the Island.* Avalon, CA: DESK Enterprises, 2003.

Miller, Ray, and Jo Miller. *Catalina: "…Wish You Were Here."* Bakersfield, CA: Sierra Printers Inc., 1993.

Millspaugh, Charles Frederick, and Lawrence William Nuttall. *The Flora of Santa Catalina Island.* Chicago: Field Museum of Natural History, 1923. Reprint, Charleston, SC: Nabu Press, 2011.

Moore, Patricia Anne. *The Casino: Catalina Island's "Two Million Dollar Palace of Pleasure."* 2nd ed. Avalon, CA: Catalina Island Museum Society Inc. and Philip K. Wrigley Publishing Fund, 2002.

Overholt, Alma. *The Catalina Story.* Avalon, CA: Philip K. Wrigley Fund, 1958. Reprint edited and updated by Jack Overholt, Avalon, CA: Island Press, 1976.

Pedersen, Jeannine L., and Catalina Island Museum. *Images of America: Catalina by Air.* Charleston, SC: Arcadia Publishing, 2008.

———. *Images of America: Catalina by Sea: A Transportation History.* Charleston, SC: Arcadia Publishing, 2006.

———. *Images of America: Catalina Island.* Charleston, SC: Arcadia Publishing, 2004.

Pedersen, Jeannine L., Stacey A. Otte, James Chen and the Catalina Island Museum Society Inc. *The Art of Catalina's Clay Products.* Avalon, CA: Catalina Island Museum Society Inc. and Philip K. Wrigley Publishing Fund, 2000.

Ramming, Burney. *The Story of Catalina Island.* Avalon, CA: Catalina Post Card Company, 1996.

Ramsay, Chris. *"In All the World, No Other Place Like This": A Pictorial History of Catalina.* N.p., n.d.

Rathbun, Loyd, and Chuck Liddell. *The Legends of Old Ben, 1899–192?.* Avalon, CA: Catalina Island Museum Society Inc., 1978.

Reynolds, Ann Cloud. *Canyon Trails of Catalina*. Avalon, CA: Ann Cloud Reynolds, 1950.

———. *Mountain Trails of Catalina*. Avalon, CA: Ann Cloud Reynolds, 1948.

———. *Wild Goat Trails of Catalina*. Avalon, CA: Ann Cloud Reynolds, 1941. Reprint, Whitefish, MT: Literary Licensing, LLC, 2012.

Ritter, Ema I. *Life at the Old Amphibian Airport*. Avalon, CA: Hal C. Ritter, 1970.

Rivken, Mike, and Jon Council. *Catalina Island Dive Buddies: The Indispensible Guide to What's Really Down There*. La Jolla, CA: Silverfish Press, 2013.

Robinson, W.W. *The Island of Santa Catalina*. Los Angeles: Title Guarantee & Trust Company, 1941.

Rosenthal, Lee. *Catalina in the Movies*. Sausalito, CA: Windgate Books, 2003.

———. *Catalina Tile of the Magic Isle*. Sausalito, CA: Windgate Books, 1992.

Rowland, Steven Mark. *Geology of Santa Catalina Island and Nearby Basins*. Oakdale, CA: National Association of Geology Teachers, Far West Section, 1984.

Rulli, Marti, and Dennis Davern. *Goodbye Natalie, Goodbye Splendour*. Aurora, IL: Medallion Media, 2009.

Scott, Carlton B. "Bud," ed. *Catalina Island Yacht Club: 85ʰ Anniversary, 1924–2009*. Avalon, CA: Catalina Island Yacht Club, 2009.

Smith, William Sidney Tangier. *The Geology of Santa Catalina Island*. San Francisco: California Academy of Sciences, 1897. Reprint, Charleston, SC: Nabu Press, 2010.

Spalding, Phebe Estelle. *Patron Saints of California: Santa Catalina*. Claremont, CA: Saunders Studio Press, 1934.

Stern, Jean, and Roy C. Rose, Molly Siple, Barbara Doutt, et al. *Enchanted Isle: A History of Plein Air Painting on Catalina Island*. Avalon, CA: Society for the Advancement of Plein Air Painting, 2003.

Stuart, J.N. *Catalina's Yesterdays: A Glimpse into the Life of the Ancient Dwellers of the Magic Isle*. Los Angeles: Mayers Company, 1926.

Vander Velde, Nancy. *What Just Flew By?: A Guide to Catalina's Birds*. Avalon, CA: Catalina Marine, 1980.

Vitti, Jim. *The Cubs on Catalina: A Scrapbook of Memories About a 30-Year Love Affair Between One of Baseball's Classic Teams…and California's Most Fanciful Isle*. Darien, CT: Settefrati Press, 2003.

———. *Images of Baseball: Chicago Cubs, Baseball on Catalina Island*. Charleston, SC: Arcadia Publishing, 2010.

Walters, Chris. *Catalina Island Fresh Fish Cook Book*. Two Harbors, CA: West End Publishing, 1991.

Watson, Jim. *Mysterious Island: Catalina, The Strange Side of Catalina*. Avalon, CA: Channel Catalina, 2012.

White, William Sanford. *Catalina Goes to War: World War II, 1941–1945*. Avalon, CA: White Limited Editions and White Family Trust, 2002.

White, William Sanford, and Kim Lianne Stotts. *The Wrigley Family: A Legacy of Leadership in Santa Catalina Island*. Glendora, CA: White Limited Editions, 2005.

White, William Sanford, and Steven Kern Tice. *Santa Catalina Island: Its Magic, People and History*. Glendora, CA: White Limited Editions, 2000.

Wicklund, Bruce. *Boat, Dive and Fish Catalina Island*. Avalon, CA: Black Dolphin Diving, 2005.

Wilson, Harry. *Wilson's Guide to Avalon the Beautiful, and the Island of Santa Catalina*. Washington, D.C.: Library of Congress, 1913. Reprint, Ulan Press, 2012.

Windle, Ernest. *History of Santa Catalina Island*. Avalon, CA: Catalina Islander Press, 1931. Reprinted and updated as *Windle's History of Santa Catalina Island*. Avalon, CA, 1940, 1949.

Wlodarski, Robert James, and Anne Nathan-Wlodarski. *Haunted Catalina: A History of the Island and Guide to Paranormal Activity*. West Hills, CA: G-Host Publishing, 1996.

Secondary Historical Sources

Batman, Richard. *The Outer Coast*. San Diego: Harcourt, 2002.

Culver, Lawrence. *The Frontier of Leisure: Southern California and the Shaping of Modern America*. New York: Oxford University Press, 2010.

Flaherty, Joseph S. *Those Powerful Years: The South Coast and Los Angeles, 1887–1917*. Hicksville, NY: Exposition Press, 1987. Reprint, Los Angeles: Historical Society of Southern California, 1992.

Ginsberg, Joanne S., et al., and the California Coastal Commission. *California Coastal Resource Guide*. Berkeley: University of California Press, 1987.

Marquez, Ernest, and Veronique Turenne. *Port of Los Angeles: An Illustrated History, 1850–1945*. Santa Monica, CA: Angel City Press, 2007.

McCawley, William. *The First Angelinos: The Gabrielino Indians of Los Angeles*. Banning, CA: Ballena Press, 1996.

Miller, Bruce W. *The Gabrielino*. Los Osos, CA: Sand River Press, 1993.

Queenan, Charles F. *The Port of Los Angeles: From Wilderness to World Port*. San Pedro, CA: Los Angeles Harbor Department, 1983.

Sitton, Tom. *Grand Ventures: The Banning Family and the Shaping of Southern California*. San Marino, CA: Huntington Library Press, 2010.

Vickery, Oliver. *Harbor Heritage: Tales of the Harbor Area of Los Angeles, California*. Mountain View, CA: Authors Book Company, 1979.

Some Books on the Channel Islands

Daily, Marla. *California's Channel Islands: 1,001 Questions Answered.* Santa Barbara, CA: McNally & Loftin, Publishers, 1987.

Daily, Marla, and Santa Cruz Island Foundation. *Images of America: The California Channel Islands.* Charleston, SC: Arcadia Publishing, 2012.

Doran, Adelaide LeMert. *Pieces of Eight Channel Islands: A Bibliographical Guide and Source Book.* Glendale, CA: Arthur H. Clark Company, 1980.

Gleason, Duncan. *Islands and Ports of California.* New York: Devin-Adair Company, 1958.

Hillinger, Charles. *The California Islands.* Los Angeles: Academy Publishing, 1958.

———. *Charles Hillinger's Channel Islands.* Santa Barbara, CA: Santa Cruz Island Foundation, 1999.

Holder, Charles Frederick. *The Channel Islands of California: A Book for the Angler, Sportsman, and Tourist.* 1910. Reprint, Ithaca, NY: Cornell University Press, 2010.

Miller, Max. *"…And Bring All Your Folks."* New York: Doubleday & Company, 1959. Republished as *A Personal Guide to California's Secret Islands.* New York: Ballantine Books, 1972.

Books on Geographic Nomenclature

Gudde, Edwin G., and William Bright. *California Place Names: The Origin and Etymology of Current Geographical Names.* 4th ed. Berkeley: University of California Press, 1998.

Hanna, Phil Townsend. *The Dictionary of California Land Names.* Los Angeles: Automobile Club of Southern California, 1946.

Secondary Natural History Sources

Bakus, Gerald J. *Natural History of Santa Catalina Island.* Denver: Outskirts Press Inc., 2011.

Bandini, Ralph. *Veiled Horizons: Stories of Big Game Fish of the Sea.* New York: Derrydale Press, 1939.

Beans, Bruce E. *Eagle's Plume: Preserving the Life and Habitat of America's Bald Eagle.* New York: Scribner, 1996.

Coonan, Timothy J., Catherin A. Schwemm and David K. Garcelon. *Decline and Recovery of the Island Fox: A Case Study for Population Recovery: Ecology, Biodiversity and Conservation.* Cambridge, UK: Cambridge University Press, 2010.

Harden, Deborah. *California Geology.* Upper Saddle River, NJ: Prentice Hall, 2003.

Hogue, Charles L. *Insects of the Los Angeles Basin.* Los Angeles: Natural History Museum of Los Angeles County, 1993.

Holder, Charles Frederick. *Big Game Fishes of the United States.* New York: Macmillan Publishers (American Sportsman's Library), 1903.

———. *Fishes of the Pacific Coast: A Handbook for Sportsmen and Tourists.* Reprint, Charleston, SC: BiblioBazaar, 2010.

———. *Salt Water Game Fishing.* New York: Outing Publishing Company, 1914.

Howell, A.B. *Birds of the Islands off the Coast of Southern California.* Hollywood, CA: University of California, 1917.

McPhee, John. *Assembling California.* New York: Farrar, Straus & Giroux, 1994.

Quammen, David. *The Song of the Dodo: Island Biogeography in an Age of Extinction.* New York: Scribner Publishing, 2011.

Secondary Biography

Angle, Paul M. *Philip K. Wrigley: A Memoir of a Modest Man.* Chicago: Rand McNally & Company, 1975.

Axelrod, Alan. *Patton: A Biography.* London: Palgrave Macmillan, 2006.

Gruber, Frank. *Zane Grey: A Biography.* New York: World Publishing, 1970.

Kelsey, Harry. *Juan Rodriguez Cabrillo.* San Marino, CA: Huntington Library Press, 1998.

Krythe, Maymie. *Port Admiral: Phineas Banning, 1830–1885.* San Francisco: California Historical Society, 1957.

Newmark, Harris. *Sixty Years in California, 1853–1913.* New York: Knickerbocker Press, 1916.

Pauly, Thomas H. *Zane Grey: His Life, His Adventures, His Women.* Urbana: University of Illinois Press, 2005.

Shaler, William. *Journal of a Voyage Between China and the North-Western Coast of America, Made in 1804.* Claremont, CA: Saunders Studio Press, 1935.

Walker, Bob. *Ultimate Diving Adventures: Adventure Stories for Scuba Divers, Thrill Seekers and Risk Takers.* Charleston, SC: CreateSpace, 2012.

Wilson, Carol Green, ed. *William R. Staats, Business Pioneer.* Whitefish, MT: Kessinger Publishing, 2005.

Wright, Helen. *James Lick's Monument: The Saga of Captain Richard Floyd and the Building of the Lick Observatory.* Cambridge, UK: Cambridge University Press, 2003.

Zimmerman, William. *William Wrigley, Jr., the Man and His Business, 1861–1932.* Chicago: R.R. Donnelly & Sons at the Lakeside Press, 1935.

Pamphlets, Reports and Other Items of Interest

Coulter, Harry. *Catalina: The Beguiling Isle.* Los Angeles: Southern California Automobile Club News, 1965.

French, Dwight G. *Fishing at Santa Catalina Island: Its Development and Methods.* Quarterly of the Department of Fish and Game. Vol. II. 1914.

Gilbert, Charles H. *Report on Fishes Obtained by the Steamer Albatross in the Vicinity of Santa Catalina Island and Monterey Bay.* Sacramento: Fish Commissioner Report, George M. Bowers, Commissioner, 1898.

Hilscher, Ralph. *In the Matter of the Application of the Santa Catalina Island Company, Avalon, for Permit to Discharge Septic Tank Effluent Through Submerged Outlet into the Pacific Ocean.* Sacramento: State of California, Department of Public Health, Engineering Division, 1919.

Pedersen, Jeannine L., and Catalina Island Museum. *Postcards of America: Catalina Island: 15 Historic Postcards.* Charleston, SC: Arcadia Publishing, 2010.

Preston, E.B. *Santa Catalina Island, Los Angeles County.* Annual Report. Vol. X. California Division of Mines and Geology, State Mining Bureau, 1891.

Reider, M. *Santa Catalina Island.* Los Angeles, 1905.

Roalfe, George Adams. *Quarrying and Crushing Methods and Costs at the Santa Catalina Island Quarry of Graham Bros., Inc..* Santa Catalina Island, CA, 1932.

Santa Catalina Island: California's Magic Isle. Wilmington, CA: Wilmington Transportation Company, 1925.

Santa Catalina Island Company, Pottery Division. *Catalina Pottery.* Los Angeles: Delleen Enge, 1988.*Santa Catalina Island: Things to See and Do.* Avalon, CA: Santa Catalina Island Company, 1933.

Tucker, W. Burling. *Mineral Resources of Santa Catalina Island.* Annual Report. Vol. X. California Division of Mines and Geology, State Mining Bureau, 1927.

Williams, Iza. *Santa Catalina Island, 1905.* Avalon, CA: Wall Enterprises, n.d.

Wilmington Transportation Company. *Catalina Island: In All the World, No Trip Like This.* Avalon, CA: Santa Catalina Island Company, 1931.

Wlodarski, Robert James. *A Bibliography of Catalina Island Investigations and Excavations (1850–1980).* Los Angeles: Institute of Archaeology, University of California–Los Angeles, 1982.

Periodicals

Avalon Bay News
Catalina Islander
In Room Magazine (*Catalina Islander* publication)
Long Beach Press-Telegram
Los Angeles Times

BIBLIOGRAPHY

New York Times
(San Pedro, CA) News-Pilot
(Torrance, CA) Daily Breeze

Websites

Americanjourneys.org
Ancestory.com
Catalina.com
Catalinabiblechurch.info
Catalinaconservancy.org
Catalina Islander Archive
Digitallibrary.usc.com
Examiner.com
Findagrave.com
LAmag.com
LATimes.com
Militarymuseum.org
Movies.broadwayworld.com
Naturespeace.org
Openwaterswimming.com
Parks.ca.gov
Parks.ca.org
Rain.org
Sandiegohistory.org
Sportillustrated.cnn.com
Visiticatalinaisland.com
Zanegreyinc.com

Documentary Films/Videos

Miller, Danny, writer/director. *Catalina: A Treasure From the Past.* 1996.
Watson, Jim, writer/director. *Wings Across the Channel: Catalina Island's Aviation History, 1946-Present.* 2010.

INDEX

INDEX

ABOUT THE AUTHORS

PATRICIA J. MAXWELL is the director of marketing and communications for the Catalina Island Conservancy. She has been producer of the Isla Earth Radio Series for the conservancy since 2006. She formerly was director of media relations for the Natural History Museum of Los Angeles County and a syndicated science and education columnist for several Los Angeles newspapers.

BOB RHEIN formerly was the media relations news writer for the Catalina Island Conservancy. He began writing as a cub reporter and photographer with the *Fullerton Daily News Tribune*, an afternoon newspaper, in the days of iron men and wooden typewriters. Rhein worked for the Natural History Museum of Los Angeles County before joining the conservancy in 2004 to call attention to the Catalina Island fox's recovery from near extinction.

JERRY ROBERTS is the senior editor and writer for the Catalina Island Conservancy and a commissioning editor for The History Press. Formerly an acquisitions editor for Arcadia Publishing and film critic of the former Copley Los Angeles Newspapers, he is the author or editor of eighteen books, including *Hollywood Scandal Almanac*; *The Complete History of American Film Criticism*; *Mitchum: In His Own Words*; *The Great American Playwrights on the Screen*; and the young adult biography *Roberto Clemente*.

Visit us at
www.historypress.net
···
This title is also available as an e-book